The classic Jaguar saloons

The classic Jaguar saloons

A collector's guide
by Chris Harvey

MOTOR RACING PUBLICATIONS LTD
28 Devonshire Road, Chiswick, London W4 2HD, England

ISBN 0 900549 59 9
First published 1981

Photosetting by Zee Creative Ltd., London SW16
Printed in Great Britain by The Garden City Press Ltd.,
Letchworth, Hertfordshire SG6 1JS

Contents

The birthplace of all classic Jaguar saloons since 1952 at Brown's Lane, Allesley, near Coventry. Here, two lines of Mark VII saloons, interspersed with the occasional XK 120 two-seater, travel down the assembly tracks while a further line of XKs take shape in the opposite direction.

Introduction

I count myself fortunate to be able to recall so many thousands of pleasurable miles behind the wheel of some of the cars featured in this Collector's Guide. Yet perhaps my most vivid memory is of an occasion long before I was old enough to hold a driving licence. I was making one of my many perilous journeys across a busy London street, dashing in and out of the traffic and somehow just managing to dodge all the cars, trucks, buses and taxis, when suddenly I stopped dead in my tracks. So, it seemed, did much of the traffic, fortunately without colliding. The cause of the sudden hiatus was probably the most graceful saloon car ever to have been driven down that piece of road. I had just had my first sight of the then brand new Jaguar Mark VII.

Five years later, I remember battling through a snowstorm on my bicycle to ride out of Peterborough towards the Great North Road to watch the Monte Carlo Rally cars rush past. The first car on the road in the rally convoy was a Jaguar, and again it was a model I had not seen previously. This was my first sight of a Mark 1 saloon.

Ten years were to pass by before I could afford my first Jaguar — one of the fearsome 3.8-litre Mark 2 saloons, modified by Coombs. This was the first time I had ever driven a Jaguar, but for the next two years I spent much of my life in that car as I travelled the length and breadth of Britain as a newspaper reporter.

An E-type sports car and a Daimler 2½-litre saloon eventually replaced it. The Daimler was a delight — it was so smooth and silent, and it handled so delicately after the raucous, muscle-building Coombs saloon. Only another Daimler could replace it, and this time it was to be a Sovereign, which seemed to spend much of its life sweeping down to the South of France.

A further 10 years passed by before I met Graig Hinton, the man with more Jaguar saloons than I would care to count. He lent me a 420 G for a wonderful weekend of unashamed luxury while my incapacitated sports car was repaired. The only thing that surpassed the 420 G, in my view, was his convertible version, which was something out of the Great Gatsby.

It was Graig who helped me so much with this book, along with Paul Skilleter, who produced so many priceless historical pictures. He, in turn, was assisted greatly by Andrew Whyte, who used to be Jaguar's public relations manager before he switched to journalism and authorship, while I have benefitted from the help of Alan Hodge and Dave Crisp, who have replaced Andrew at Jaguar.

Another great Jaguar enthusiast, John Williams, took many of the new pictures for this book, for which I am most grateful, as I am to Warren Allport of *Autocar,* Jim Lee of *Motor* and John Dunbar and Kathy Ager of London Art Technical, who helped me secure many more. My sincere thanks, too, to so many people at Jaguar for giving us such wonderful cars, and to my publisher, John Blunsden, for enabling me to write a book about such collectable classics.

January 1981   CHRIS HARVEY

The classic status of SS and Jaguar cars has often been achieved as much by their competition successes as by their road-going specification. This is a late-model SS1 — the car which established the company as a car manufacturer rather than a coachbuilder — being put through a driving test at Brooklands.

CHAPTER 1

Ancestors and parentage

SS 1 to Mark V

Jaguar has become one of the most glorious names in British motor manufacturing, not only because of the firm's spectacularly successful sports cars, but also because of the unparalleled performance, styling and incredible value for money presented by their saloon cars. The SS and Jaguar cars made before World War 2 and immediately after were in a similar mould, but they never achieved the heady status of the cars that followed because they lacked what was to become one of the world's greatest engines, the twin-overhead-camshaft Jaguar XK unit. The Jaguar and Daimler saloons made with this engine from 1950 to 1969, when the current XJ6 took over, were the absolute classics; beloved of businessmen, racing drivers and even bank robbers, they were so far ahead of their competitors in both performance and comfort. Nor are they dead yet, for their influence and many of their components live on in the Daimler limousine which continues to compete in the top end of the luxury market.

But cars and great reputations in the motor industry are not made in a day, so how did Jaguar come to take the saloon car world by storm in 1950? It is a remarkably short story by comparison with those of some motor manufacturers, starting as recently as 1921, whereas for Daimler, who were taken over by Jaguar in 1960, it had started with the foundations of the British motor industry in 1896.

The first Jaguars-to-be were not, in fact, cars at all. They were sidecars built in Stockport, Cheshire, by one William Walmsley. His motorcycle sidecars were of unusually elegant design and they soon attracted the attention of another young enthusiast, William Lyons, when Walmsley's family moved to Blackpool, in Lancashire. Soon, Walmsley and Lyons, with financial support from their families, started producing their sidecars in quantity for an appreciative market, and they formed the Swallow Sidecar Company in 1922.

A period of expansion followed with Walmsley and Lyons sharing equal authority on the shopfloor and in the overall direction of the company. When it came to public exposure, however, Walmsley proved to be the more retiring of the partners, invariably leaving Lyons to be the spokesman. Such was the success of Walmsley's brilliant styling — an art that Lyons rapidly picked up — and their joint efforts at effective economies in construction, which kept costs to a minimum, that business boomed and the emergent manufacturer had expanded into the construction of car bodies by 1926.

Larger premises were acquired in Blackpool, and their first car bodies — mounted on Austin 7, then Morris Cowley chassis — proved to be as popular as the sidecars. People were willing to pay more for special-bodied small cars that looked totally different from their often ungainly standard-bodied counterparts. Skilled labour had to be recruited from the Midlands — the home of the British car industry — to supplement the local talent. Naturally, producing car bodies needed more room, and it was at this point that the partners decided that the future of the company, which had been renamed the Swallow Sidecar and Coachbuilding Company in 1927, lay with cars rather than sidecars.

Although coachbuilding meant bigger overheads, it also meant bigger profits and offered a better future as the popularity of light cars as family transport overtook that of the motorcycle combination. By 1928, the need for larger premises had become acute; in addition, money was being wasted, in effect, by having

Sir William Lyons and his wife, Lady Lyons. The Chairman of Jaguar often proved to be a most demanding test driver of his company's products.

respectively — that they were a great success. Like the Swallow-bodied cars before them, they also featured brilliant colour schemes, rather than the austere black favoured by so many manufacturers of that period. It was a brave new venture during the depths of an economic depression that succeeded because of the combination of brilliant styling and an extraordinarily low price. One of the ways in which Lyons kept down the price — Walmsley was soon to move on to caravan manufacture — was by planning for long production runs, whereas so many rivals in those days changed their models annually, which meant that extra costs were incurred by the disturbance to production lines and the need for new tools and jigs. The change in emphasis towards car production was underlined in 1933 by the registration of a new company, SS Cars Ltd.

The performance of SS cars had been improved considerably by 1934 with the help of larger engines by Standard, and a further leap forward took place in 1935 with the introduction of an overhead-valve conversion by Harry Weslake for the 2,664 cc Standard unit to power the six-cylinder model in a stylish new range of saloons called SS Jaguars — the first time the marque had used the name that was to become world famous. In 1937, new bodies were announced, made entirely from steel, rather than by the heavier and more expensive traditional method of using metal panels on a wooden frame, and by the following year three engine sizes were being marketed of 1,776 cc, 2,664 cc and 3,485 cc, to power models catalogued as 1½-litre, 2½-litre and 3½-litre versions of the same basic design.

Like all Lyons' previous products, the price was kept to a minimum by the use of highly organized, streamlined production lines. The late-1930s were also significant in that they heralded a boom in the export business because of the outstandingly good value for money offered by the new SS Jaguars. By then the manufacture of Swallow sidecars had been hived-off to a separate company.

SS Cars made aircraft parts and experimental jeeps during the war and changed their name to Jaguar Cars Ltd just before hostilities ended in 1945 because their initials at that time had become so closely associated with all that was most hated in Nazi Germany. The company also relinquished their residual interest in sidecars and concentrated solely on cars, with the emphasis on exports. This was necessary to ensure supplies of steel, which

to transport the finished chassis to Blackpool, in the North of England, from the Midlands, so that the Swallow bodies could be fitted. Furthermore, there were more skilled workers available in the Midlands, so it was decided to move south. A works was secured at Foleshill, Coventry, in 1928 and soon other makers' chassis were being used, including those of Standard. It was a Standard chassis that was to form the basis of Lyons' first complete car, the SS 1, in 1931. It could justly be called a complete car because the Standard chassis and engine were made specially for the SS rather than the new car being simply a Standard with a special Swallow body. The SS 1, and a smaller version called the SS 2, were long, low, rakish saloons which looked so good and cost so little — just over £300 and £200, could be released in quantity only to foreign currency-earning manufacturers. By 1947, the first left-hand-drive Jaguar saloons and drop-head coupes were being exported to the United States, these being based on the prewar SS Jaguar models and generally referred to, retrospectively, as Mark IVs.

These were only stopgap cars, however, on the way to the Jaguars that would soon take the world by storm. Work on the new car had started before the war when independent front suspension was tested on a 3½-litre saloon. This new system was essential for a car of advanced technology to replace the time-

The SS 1, which marked the transition from coachbuilding to complete car manufacture, was produced in several body styles. This is a later coupe, with full wings and running boards and more rounded radiator and windscreen, which was produced from 1933.

honoured cart-sprung front axle which suffered from the deficiencies of inferior roadholding and ride. Jaguar's independent front suspension was designed by their chief engineer, William Heynes, who had joined the company from Humber in 1935. It was based on the torsion bar-and-wishbone arrangement used on the revolutionary *Traction Avant* Citroen of 1934 — the car that was later to be made famous throughout the world as the *Maigret* police car. Heynes' innovation in this system was to use ball-joints to carry the stub-axle — a brilliant, cheap, simple and effective set-up in the true Lyons tradition. Walter Hassan, of Brooklands and Bentley fame, assisted with the development work, which extended to trying out a variation of the new suspension on one of Jaguar's war-time jeep projects.

This was one of the first stages towards the new 100-mph saloon car that Lyons intended would spearhead his attack after the war. One of the next stages was to develop a new engine. The unit that Lyons visualized had to have twin overhead camshafts — a layout synonymous with exotic racing cars and motorcycles,

12

Announced initially as a 1938 model, the 2½-litre and 3½-litre saloons were re-introduced after the war as Jaguars, the SS prefix having been dropped. When *The Autocar* tested a 3½-litre version in 1948 it achieved more than 90 mph and the magazine considered it to be 'a front-rank car'. It was known retrospectively as the Mark IV.

The Mark V Jaguar was an unusually successful compromise design incorporating a chassis intended for a later model, a power unit from an earlier car and a body developed from a prewar design. It sold well, and in 1948 *The Autocar* said: 'One wonders why it should be necessary to go further away from the sensible shapes accepted for many years past'. This car has an unusual two-colour paint finish and non-standard cutaway rear-wheel spats.

13

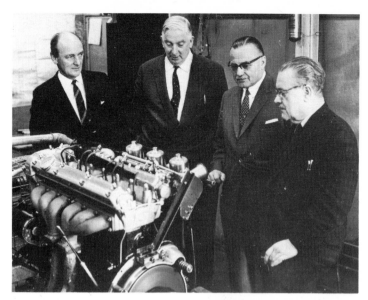

which offered the possibility of an exceptionally high power output, but had previously been considered too complicated for economic series production and maintenance by mechanics of only average ability. However, Heynes and Hassan were persuaded that they could make it work, and so was Lyons' new engine man Claude Baily, who had joined them from Morris on the outbreak of war. Mind you, they took some convincing at first, but Lyons proved as persuasive as ever and they all worked with a will during those famous and often-chronicled fire-watching sessions at the factory in wartime Coventry. Weslake helped with the vital gas-flowing of the cylinder-head and, after early experiments with four-cylinder versions of the engine, the classic six-cylinder XK unit was born in 1948.

Not only did Lyons influence its internal design, but he insisted that it should be outwardly as elegant and attractive as the bodywork of his cars. The result was a magnificently-sculptured unit with those long and highly polished cam covers which were to make so many subsequent Jaguar cars look so impressive under the bonnet.

To complete preparations for the new saloon, Lyons had an

The men behind the Jaguar XK power unit. From the left: Harry Mundy, Walter Hassan, William Heynes and Claude Baily.

With Walter Hassan beside him, William Heynes behind the wheel of one of his finest products, the XK 120 roadster, the first car to feature the famous twin-overhead-camshaft engine which was destined to power so many classic Jaguar saloons.

The elegantly engineered and very robust torsion-bar independent front suspension and steering mechanism designed by William Heynes for the Mark VII but first used on the Mark V models. This picture shows a left-hand-drive installation.

improved, stiffer chassis designed to take the independent front suspension and the XK engine. Needless to say, he also had a new body in mind, but it could not be put into production in conjunction with the other components because, for the first time, the company was having to buy its bodyshells from an outside supplier. This was because of the size of the panels needed for the new body, which could not be built economically by the old methods. Tooling-up for such a shell took a year or more, so, in the meantime, Lyons and Heynes considered how best the existing range of Mark IV Jaguars could benefit from a spot of revitalization.

Preparations for production of the new engine were nearly as complicated as those demanded by the new body, so it was decided to start with the new chassis, fitting it with only the existing 2½-litre and 3½-litre engines because the 1½-litre (1,776 cc) unit would not give the heavier new car sufficient performance. A new body was designed along the traditional lines so that it could be build up piecemeal at Foleshill while the works were waiting for the larger-panelled shell. This car, with its new front suspension, interim body and old engine, was the Mark V Jaguar and it was produced in saloon and drop-head coupe form; it was an elegant, although somewhat dated, car that sold well in the two years from 1948.

Meanwhile, Lyons decided to try out the new XK engine in a shortened version of the new chassis, clothing the result with a spectacular sports car body. This was the sensational Jaguar XK 120 that was to cost less than £1,000 and looked and performed more like a £4,000 Ferrari, of which only a handful were made. During an early publicity run, the new XK 120 touched 132 mph (with slight modifications) and almost overnight Jaguar was the name on all motorists' lips. Lyons intended only a short run of the new sports car, while he prepared for the new saloon — which was to be the mainstay of production — but such was the demand that he extended the life of the XK range for another 13 years! Meanwhile, the world was wondering what he had in store with the new saloon and they were not to be disappointed by the Mark VII that was to be unveiled in 1950. It was called the Mark VII rather than the Mark VI (in logical sequence) to avoid confusion with Bentley, whose standard model was already called the Mark VI. The Bentley cost a fortune, but it could not rival the Jaguar on performance, let alone price, and it scored only marginally on coachwork, but not on lines. The Jaguar Mark VII, the subject of the next chapter, along with its derivatives, was to be Lyons' first world-beating saloon.

CHAPTER 2

The Mark VII, VIII and IX

1950 to 1961

Grace, Space and Pace were the three words from the advertising world which symbolized the car that was to lay the foundations for Jaguar's continuing prosperity as a car manufacturer, the Mark VII saloon. It was certainly graceful, with a voluptuous appeal that was held in check by the slender lines of Lyons' good taste; it was certainly spacious, as anybody who has wallowed in the luxurious leather of a Mark VII can testify — up to six people could be accommodated in comfort; and it certainly had pace, thanks to its wonderful XK engine, which achieved Lyons' aim of hauling this large car along at more than the magic 100 mph. Because it had a long stroke, it produced not only ample power, but also excellent torque, which endowed the Mark VII with remarkable acceleration. It was a practical pace, too, because the new chassis worked so well. It was more rigid than that used before, with softer suspension which offered better roadholding with a ride that was immeasurably superior.

The chassis was massive, as befitted a car that would weigh more than two tons fully laden. Two 6.5-inch deep box-section side-members ran parallel to the ground from the front of the chassis to just before the back axle, where they were swept sharply over it before being extended to take the rear spring hangers. These 3.5-inch wide 14-swg steel side-members were tapered at either end to reduce weight and were liberally braced with channel-section cross-members and box-sections at the front and rear. The torsion bars from the front suspension's wishbones ran alongside the chassis side-members, with telescopic shock absorbers located on the bottom wishbones and on brackets above the chassis. Metalistik bonded rubber bushes were used extensively in the suspension mountings to reduce noise,

harshness and vibration. An anti-roll bar linking the two bottom suspension members — which were triangulated to make effective wishbones — had a mounting under the front chassis cross-member.

The rear suspension followed conventional practice with half-elliptic leaf springs either side, but it differed from that fitted to Jaguars designed prewar in that the chassis, which now went over the axle, allowed more suspension movement without the bottoming that would have been experienced with the underslung chassis. The rear springs were 6 inches longer than those used on the Mark IV and softer, which, in combination with the more rigid chassis, gave better roadholding and ride. Lever-arm shock absorbers were mounted on the chassis side-members ahead of the Salisbury rear axle.

The engine was that magnificent piece of work which had already been introduced in the race-winning XK 120 sports car. It had the now-classic dimensions of an 83 mm bore and 106 mm stroke giving a capacity of 3,442 cc. Two compression ratios were available, 8:1 and 7:1. In 8:1 form it produced 160 bhp at 5,200 rpm and 195 lb ft of torque at 2,500 rpm — more than any contemporary production engine other than the Cadillac V8. The lower compression ratio version, which was intended for areas which still did not have good-quality fuel, produced only 10 bhp less. The chief source of so much power was the alloy cylinder-head, which dispersed heat more easily than a cast-iron head (which would have weighed 120 lb against the alloy head's 50 lb); it was the world's first hemispherical twin-overhead-camshaft design to go into volume production. Its seven-bearing crankshaft with massive 2.75-inch bearings was practically indestructible and its cast-iron block was relatively light because it did not have to contain the camshafts — which were chain-driven — and was strong in all the right places because it had been designed without compromise. It had a low-pressure lubrication system to reduce power-sapping oil drag and the lightweight valve gear was operated direct from the camshafts through bucket tappets to ensure the highest efficiency. The bores proved to be sufficiently hard-wearing when a chromed top piston ring was used to obviate the need for cylinder liners. The only compromises apart from a rather long stroke — which at least had the benefit of giving that excellent torque — were to be seen in the two chains used to drive the cams (which were quieter than a single chain) and the fitting of 0.3125-inch cams, rather than the preferred type with 0.375-inch lift, to avoid the possibility of backyard mechanics bending the valves when turning the cams during decokes — still quite a common operation in 1950.

Two 1.75-inch SU carburettors were fitted, with one SU electric fuel pump for each of the two petrol tanks, which were

Driver's-eye view of an early XK engine with its 'tall' SU carburettors before their shape was changed to a squatter profile and additional studs were added to the engine's camshaft covers to make it more oil-tight.

The Mark VII's substantial chassis can be clearly seen in this picture taken at Brown's Lane with nearly-completed cars lined up in the background.

mounted in each rear wing to give as much space as possible for luggage. The carburettors were augmented by an automatic electric starting device that was frequently fitted with a manual override switch by owners dissatisfied with the autocratic way in which it worked (it often stayed on longer than needed, being set to provide a safety-first mixture sufficiently rich to enable the engine to be started in the coldest of climates).

The new Mark VII saloon was the star of the show when it was introduced at the Waldorf-Astoria hotel in Park Avenue, New York, in 1950. More than 500 orders were taken in the first three days it was on display.

The Mark VII saloon's brake servo vacuum tank can be seen in this picture of a partly-completed chassis, as can the adjuster for one of the front suspension's torsion-bars.

The power was harnessed by a 10-inch single-dry-plate Borg and Beck clutch that seldom gave any trouble, despite the weight of the vehicle. It was hydraulically operated on all but the first 55 cars. The four-speed gearbox was also exceptionally strong, with synchromesh on the top three ratios. The ratios of 14.4, 8.48, 5.84 and 4.27:1 were wider than those on the XK 120 sports car in view of the weight and bulk of the saloon, but the XK 120 gearbox could be substituted for improved performance in competition. The wider ratios were preferable, however, if the Mark VII's carrying capacity was to be used to the full. These gearboxes, although rather slow and ponderous to use by modern standards, were considered quite acceptable in 1950, despite the long movement needed to change gear.

The gearbox was connected to the hypoid-bevel rear axle by a Hardy-Spicer propeller-shaft, divided to allow a flat floor to be fitted — another way in which the passenger space inside the car was improved. An axle ratio of 4.27:1 was employed, although a 4.55:1 could be substituted for maximum acceleration. The lower ratio was usually fitted for competition use, enabling the bulky car to reach its maximum attainable speed on a track more quickly than with the standard ratio.

Braking was beginning to become a problem with most cars built since the war. Before the war, large, narrow wheels had been commonplace with wings that hardly shrouded them; the Mark IV Jaguars, for instance, had 18-inch wire wheels. As a result, the

An exposed view of a rear brake of a Mark VII also showing the gaitered rear spring with grease nipple on top at the left.

brake drums were exposed to ample cooling air and there was plenty of room for the heat generated by braking to be expelled through the spoked wheels and out of the wings. After the war, more efficient, streamlined bodies had become the order of the day, with smaller and more economical steel disc wheels. The Mark V Jaguar, for example, had 16-inch steel wheels, which were carried over to the Mark VII and which reduced the unsprung weight of the car and lowered its centre of gravity. They were also more rigid and resulted in better roadholding; they were cheaper to make and needed no maintenance, unlike spoked wheels; and they were also far easier to keep clean. The only things to really suffer from the change to smaller steel wheels

were the brakes, which no longer received sufficient cooling air, while the new wheels and all-enveloping wings hindered the dispersal of the heat generated by braking. In addition, the diameter of the brake drums often had to be reduced because of the smaller wheel size, and as a result a smaller area of friction material had to cope with greater braking stresses, particularly on cars such as Jaguars, which were becoming so much faster.

These problems, which manifested themselves in complete brake fade as the linings overheated, caused Jaguars to fit a new system on the Mark VII. The front drums, which had to take most of the strain, were fitted with two trailing shoes rather than the more conventional two leading shoes. The trouble with the

The hydraulic assembly used to operate the clutch on all but the first few Mark VII saloons can be seen alongside the gearbox and bellhousing in this partly-assembled rolling chassis. The gearbox oil level dipstick — accessible through a carpet-covered hole in the floor of a completed car — can be seen on the left.

Four stages in the creation of the Jaguar Mark VII. The front view of an early mock-up shows a flat one-piece windscreen from a Mark V being used with a new radiator grille narrowed in the manner of the grille of the XK 120 sports car. The sidelight fittings are similar to those of the sports car and were to be retained on the saloon. The left-hand side of the experimental body shows a wide bonnet line extending into the wings, but this was not to be adopted on a production Jaguar during the 1950s. However, the bonnet line on the other side eventually saw service in the Mark 1 saloon of 1955. The large enclosed headlight never found favour on a Jaguar saloon, neither did the built-in indicator arrows, although they were soon to be used on buses; the large headlight eventually found a home on a lorry. It was clear, however, that the front wing lines of the Mark VII were already taking

shape. In the second picture, the body is much closer to the eventual Mark VII shape, particularly in the roof and window lines, which bear a strong resemblance at the back to those of the Mark V saloon. The rear wing lines are already well established, but the front wings bear a close resemblance to those used on the rival contemporary saloon made by Bentley. In the third picture, the bodylines are so near completion that the shell has been assembled on a Mark V saloon chassis rather than on the wooden trestles used for the earlier two mock-ups. At this point the car would undergo a road test and then would be taken to the Lyons home, Wappenbury Hall, for surveillance in natural surroundings, well away from any vestige of the factory; you could say that the boss was taking his work home with him! The fourth picture shows the eventual product, in its North American export guise.

two-leading-shoe system was that the layout of the shoes caused a self-servo, or binding effect, which was fine for applications where there was sufficient cooling, but once the linings went beyond their heat barrier their efficiency faded and when they cooled down again they frequently worked unevenly. Greater pedal pressures were needed with the trailing-shoe brakes so a servo was incorporated in the system. This was a Clayton-Dewandre unit, which used the vacuum created by the engine's inlet manifold to produce around double the normal hydraulic pressure. It was made fail-safe in that if something went wrong with the servo — or the engine cut out — the brakes still worked by direct action, although they were heavier to operate, of course. The shoes in the front brakes were also self-adjusting, which helped tremendously as the linings and drums heated-up.

Twelve-inch drums were fitted all round, using the existing one-leading and one-trailing shoe system at the back. These shoes were also operated by the handbrake mechanism, the lever being located on the floor between the front seats. Although this system was a great improvement on the one used earlier, it was still possible to induce fade on a hard-driven Mark VII, but this was not considered a serious shortcoming in the early-1950s, when many similar cars, particularly those made in America, suffered far worse!

The steering gear also fell into this category. A Burman recirculating-ball, worm-and-nut system was used, geared down to 4.75 turns from lock to lock. This was considered to be rather slow by the British, but suited the American market well as customers there were accustomed at that time to driving cars with

Jaguar Mark VIIs even attracted world championship Grand Prix drivers. On the left is Dr. Giuseppe Farina, who won the title with Alfa Romeo in 1950, the year in which the picture was taken. Next to him is his close rival and fellow Italian Alberto Ascari, who was to become world champion in 1952 and 1953 with Ferrari.

five turns from lock to lock. It was obvious where Jaguar's priorities lay, but they managed to avoid the dead feeling forever associated with the steering of American cars of that period. The Mark VII's steering was acceptably light on the move, but there was some criticism that it proved heavy for parking, particularly from women. The tyres tended to squeal under cornering at the lowest recommended settings, 24 psi front and 27 psi rear, which gave the softest ride. It was generally considered better to inflate them to 30 psi front and 36 psi rear for the best handling, as the ride hardly suffered. Wheelspin could be provoked quite easily on slippery surfaces, but it did not cause undue problems.

The Motor magazine summed it all up by saying: 'The Jaguar is probably the best compromise yet evolved between many conflicting requirements. It provides much of the quality of finish and equipment expected on the most costly cars, at a fraction of their price. It also offers outstanding speed, with flexibility and quite a high order of silence. It provides excellent riding comfort and also a considerable degree of roadworthiness. Finally, it is extremely roomy, yet uses fuel at a rate appreciably lower than its size and speed would suggest.'

This was partly due to the good aerodynamics of the body which had been designed by Lyons. He worked in the metal rather than from a drawing board. Lyons secreted himself in a special part of the bodyshop at Foleshill with a few panel-beaters and woodworkers. They made mock-ups to his verbal instructions and sketches, then experimented with raised and lowered wing lines, different front profiles and so on until the car looked right to him. At this stage the panels would have been hung on a wooden frame which corresponded to the dimensions of wheelbase, passenger compartment size and length that had been worked out by Heynes. Only when Lyons was satisfied that everything was just right were the pattern-makers and draughtsmen called in to work direct from the prototype body.

Jaguar had neither the money nor the room for the complicated press tools needed to make a modern all-steel body like that needed for the Mark VII, so the order was given to Pressed Steel. In addition to having the equipment needed for such a large-scale operation, they had extensive experience in making such bodyshells which were to be supplied bare and transported to Foleshill ready for painting and trimming.

The car that was unveiled in October 1950 had a roof and rear

Ingenious attention to detail showed everywhere in Jaguars, not only in methods of saving money in construction, but in ways of giving the customer something extra that pleased the eye and looked expensive, yet cost little more to fit. The tool case concealed in the front door trim of the Mark VII saloon was a good example.

quarters like those of the Mark V, all soft, round curves, with a sunroof as standard. But the wings were different, high and sweeping like those of the XK 120 sports car, with spats covering the rear wheels. The Mark VII was designed without the masses of chromium plating that was so popular with American cars of that period, so it did not have to be changed every year to give a 'new look'. This all helped to keep down production costs; once the Mark VII mould was cast it was to stay that way for as long as possible.

The engine was mounted 5 inches further forward in the chassis than it had been in the Mark V in order to make the passenger compartment as large as possible. Three of the extra inches were devoted to increasing the leg room in the back. Rear passengers also benefitted from an extra 5 inches across the body because of the new full-width design rather than the narrow Mark V with running boards. The other couple of inches liberated by

moving the engine forward were taken up by moving the rear seat forward as well. This meant that the rear wheelarches hardly intruded on its width and made the luggage boot truly enormous — a tremendous attraction to the American market. A lot of careful thought went into this end of the car with the spare wheel being stowed in an upright position to leave the boot as deep as possible and allow the wheel to be removed without first having to unpack all the luggage, while by mounting the fuel tanks in the wings a long, wide and deep space was available for the stowage of cases. At nearly 2 ft 6 in deep, 4 ft long and 3 ft 8 in at its widest point, the compartment was easily as big as those of comparable American saloons, although the Mark VII's length, at 16 ft 4.5 in, was considerably shorter than the average. Its wheelbase, however, at 10 ft, was longer than that of most American cars, and its width (6 ft 1 in) was also greater with the result that it handled better with less overhanging weight, an important

The rear seating of the Mark VII saloon, seen here to advantage with the front seats removed, was both sumptuous and elegant.

consideration for a car capable of a maximum speed of 103 mph (matched by only the largest 5-litre American cars) and acceleration (0-60 mph in 13.4 sec) that was in a class of its own. So was the price, a mere £998 on introduction in the UK.

Such was the demand for the new saloon and the XK 120 sports car that the premises at Foleshill had become hopelessly cramped and inadequate by 1951. It was at this point that Jaguar managed to secure a modern factory at Brown's Lane, Allesley, on the outskirts of Coventry, which had been used by Daimler for making armoured cars during the war. It was still being used for car and bus production, but Daimler, whose main works were at Radford, Coventry, had decided to concentrate on medium-sized saloons and their needs were contracting. Jaguar, on the other hand, were glad to take over the million square feet at Brown's Lane, which is still their home today.

Lyons did not let the sheer size of the new factory go to his head, however. The economy of line and frugal approach to life where it did not affect either image or performance was evident everywhere at Brown's Lane. Offices were austere and even in the boardroom, which was also used for entertaining, there was only just enough wood panelling and carpet to go round. Decor was clinical and everything was designed for efficiency and economy.

The cars were also made more efficient as production progressed. Jaguars, particularly the sports cars with their

The cavernous luggage boot of the Mark VII Jaguar, pictured in 1952. At this stage, neither boot mat nor carpet was provided.

restricted air intakes, had gained a reputation for overheating in exceptionally hot climates. The trouble only manifested itself on the saloons if maintenance was poor, but nevertheless, the original cast-aluminium cooling fan was replaced towards the end of 1951 by a steel one which circulated at a higher speed. The cylinder-block was also modified to take a standard water heater element for use in exceptionally cold areas. People living in such countries were also apt to complain about the rather poor interior heaters fitted to Jaguar cars, but Lyons was not inclined to take much notice of them; he always wore an overcoat when the weather was cold and thought that everybody else ought to do the same!

Wherever possible, the quality of fittings was improved within reasonable price limits; in this context, two-speed windscreen wipers were fitted in 1952 with windscreen washers following

soon after. A potential source of oil leaks was eliminated by fitting additional studs to the front of the camshaft covers during the year and the valve and tappet guides were modified to allow the 0.375-inch high-performance camshafts to be fitted without changing the cylinder-head. A gearbox of improved construction was also fitted.

Uprated Girling dampers were offered as an option and fitted as standard for some countries where the combination of rough roads and the car's great weight (34.5 cwt) gave the normal shock absorbers a tough time. Stronger and wider wheels, with 5.5-inch rather than 5-inch rims, were also fitted by the end of 1952.

Jaguar were acclaimed everywhere for the quality and finish of their cars, but they did not rest on their laurels. They changed to synthetic enamel from cellulose late in 1952 and improved the interior sealing at the same time.

Jaguars were no fools when it came to publicizing their products at minimal cost, even if they did choose April 1 for record-breaking runs on the Jabbeke motorway in Belgium in 1953. The Mark VII saloon, a much-used works racing machine, covered the flying-kilometre at an average speed of 121.704 mph, with a fastest run of 122.705 mph, and the flying-mile at an average of 121.30 mph, with a best run at 121.786 mph. The XK 120 next to it did the flying-kilometre at 141.846 mph (fastest run 141.937 mph), and the flying-mile at 140.789 mph (fastest run 141.509 mph). The C-type sports-racing car, similar to the Le Mans winner that year, established a Belgian national sports car record for the unlimited-capacity class with a flying-kilometre at 148.435 mph and a flying-mile at 147.662 mph.

By 1953, Americans were beginning to expect all luxury saloons to have automatic transmission, and Jaguar could not ignore such a trend, especially as their rivals, Rolls-Royce and Bentley, were already offering the option of an automatic gear-change. It would have taken a long time and cost a lot of money to have developed their own automatic gearbox, so Jaguar decided to use a proprietory system. These all originated in America, where such gearboxes had been in general use since before the war, and as Borg-Warner's seemed best suited to the XK engine's characteristics, it was selected for the Mark VII. It was modified slightly to match the engine's torque curve, with change-up points at higher revs than would have been used on a large, slogging, American engine. A kick-down switch was fitted to the accelerator pedal, enabling the intermediate of the gearbox's three ratios to be selected at speeds below 60 mph. This performed the function of changing-down to aid acceleration when overtaking. Bottom gear could also be held to prevent the gearbox changing-up and use the engine to slow the car. The gearbox also had an anti-creep device, which built up pressure in the hydraulic lines leading to the back brakes when the car was brought to a halt. This could be released by a touch of the throttle. An American-style parking pawl, which locked the output shaft, was also fitted. A quadrant selector was mounted on the dashboard so that it did

Above, the steering wheel of the 1952 manual Mark VII is extended to the limit of its adjustment and has the original domed centre. Left, the interior of an early automatic Mark VII, with steering wheel fully retracted and the later-style horn press. Soon after, the handbrake was repositioned further to the right (or to the left on a left-hand-drive car).

not interfere with the adjustable steering column, and a bench front seat was fitted as standard on cars with automatic transmission. This enabled them to carry six people at a squeeze, three in the front and three in the back, and meant that the handbrake lever had to be relocated in umbrella-handle form under the dashboard. Unfortunately, this proved to be nothing like as efficient as the conventional lever fitted between the bucket seats on the manual-gearbox cars. Bench seats could not be fitted to these cars because the middle passenger would have obstructed the use of the gearlever, and in any case, they were usually bought by the more sporting-minded owner, who also preferred the better location afforded by individual seating. Bench-type seats were normally fitted to American cars at that time, so all automatic Mark VIIs — which went almost exclusively to America — had them as standard.

Quite a variety of tuning devices were offered for drivers who wanted extra performance. Special pistons giving a 9:1 compression ratio could be fitted in conjunction with a modified distributor and carburettors. A C-type cylinder-head, like that fitted to competition Jaguars, with oversize valves, could be substituted for the standard head, besides using 2-inch SU carburettors. Close-ratio gears, stiffer shock absorbers and springs, and a high-ratio steering box could also be supplied for competition purposes.

Telescopic dampers replaced the old, less efficient, lever-arm shock absorbers at the back on all cars from August 1953, with an extra cross-member astride the frame to take their top mounting. Minor modifications during that year included an eight-bladed fan for better cooling with a more efficient water pump and a radiator with an expansion chamber. A pressed-steel sump replaced the original cast-alloy item to cut production costs. This meant that the anti-roll-bar mountings had to be moved down to the lower wishbone arms to give sufficient clearance. The brake servo was shielded from road debris, two throttle return springs

Rear view of the Mark VIIM showing its new rear bumper with increased wrap-round. The flashing indicators were contained within the lights.

Front view of the Mark VIIM, showing the subtle styling changes. The earlier Lucas 'tripod' headlights had been replaced with a newer design, improved Lucas foglights had been repositioned with horn grilles in place of the old inset lights, flashing indicators had replaced trafficators and the bumper profile had been redesigned along simpler lines.

The Mark VIII Jaguar, showing its new radiator grille and slightly curved one-piece windscreen.

Rear view of a Mark VIII, with chrome script on the boot-lid denoting that it is an automatic-transmission model. The chrome body line, cutaway spats and dual exhaust system can also be seen on this car, which is equipped with optional chrome wheel trims.

The rear compartment of the automatic Mark VIII with one of its convenient picnic tables extended. Note the large door handle and the recessed ashtrays.

rather than one were fitted for security, and the engine's valve springs were strengthened.

The next major change to specification to be offered was the option of overdrive from January 1954. This worked on top gear only, giving more economical high-speed cruising with the standard 3.54:1 rear axle ratio, or better acceleration with a reasonably high top ratio when the optional 4.55:1 rear axle was used. Overdrive was more popular in Europe, where fuel prices were high, whereas automatic transmission — which absorbed more power and meant that the Mark VII used more petrol when it was fitted — was more popular in America where fuel consumption mattered little in those days of very cheap petrol.

Far more substantial changes were made with the introduction of the Mark VIIM model in September 1954. This had the high-lift camshafts as standard on the 8:1 compression ratio model, which was now rated at 180 bhp rather than 160 bhp. A closer-ratio gearbox was fitted now that more power was available and stiffer front torsion-bars were used to reduce roll. Various changes

The interior of an automatic Mark VIII, showing the substantial proportions of its bench seat and the highly polished wood door cappings.

In addition, decokes were not being required so often because the quality of petrol in most countries was improving.

A new type of oil pump was fitted to all engines at the same time, together with an improved crankshaft oil seal, and better timing-chain tensioners arrived soon after. The clear indicator glasses were replaced with amber ones for legal reasons in February 1955, and the rev limit warning marking on the tachometer was moved from 5,200-5,500 to 5,500-6,000 rpm with the standardization of the high-lift camshafts. The option of automatic transmission finally became available in Britain late in 1955 and immediately became popular.

The Mark VIII Jaguar was introduced in October 1956 and the majority had automatic transmission because, by then, the new 2.4-litre compact Jaguar saloon had been put into production and this model was appealing mainly to the more sporting driver. The changes distinguishing the Mark VIII from the Mark VIIM were basically similar to those which had created the Mark VIIM out of the original Mark VII, being chiefly confined to the engine and

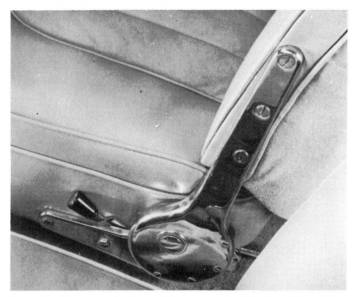

The rake adjusters on the Reutter front seats offered as an option on late-model Mark VIII Jaguars.

were made to the exterior in keeping with the revised XK 140 sports car. These included fitting new Lucas headlights, fog lights mounted outboard rather than inset, and restyled bumpers with big overriders for protection from clumsy parkers. The wheels received new rim trims and, inside the car, the old pointed horn push was replaced with a neater (and safer) flat one. The heater was modified to give more output in 1954, but there were many people who did not wear overcoats regularly who complained that it was still inadequate!

The automatic was also modified with the introduction of the Mark VIIM so that starting in 'Drive' made use of first gear rather than intermediate, to provide a brisker take-off. Soon after, a different type of Salisbury rear axle was fitted to overdrive-equipped cars.

Early in 1955, cars with the 7:1 compression ratio engine received the high-lift camshafts because it was evident that even mechanics with little knowledge of the twin-overhead-camshaft engine were coping with decokes without endangering the valves.

to styling details.

The engine had a modified C-type head, called the B-type, there being more logic behind the use of this code letter than might have been readily apparent. The original 160 bhp twin-overhead-camshaft head could now be called the A-type; the new B-type was good for 190 bhp (the same as the modified Mark VIIM head); and the C-type head was capable of producing 210 bhp. A D-type head had also been introduced for competition Jaguars in 1954 and was capable of delivering around 300 bhp. Although the B-type head produced less power than the C-type head which could optionally be fitted to a Mark VII, it endowed the Mark VIII with a far superior performance because it developed its power at lower revs. This also made it superior to the Mark VIIM's head, which developed only the same power at higher revs. The production of a B-type head involved improving the gas-flowing of the C-type head, retaining its large valves, but using the same port throats as those of the A-type head. The result, with a new twin exhaust system, was highly beneficial to the Mark VIII because high revs were rarely used by drivers of the big saloon car and the development of maximum power at lower revs was far better suited to automatic transmission.

The automatic gearbox was further modified to incorporate an intermediate speed hold worked by a switch on the dashboard. This enabled the driver to hold the middle ratio or to switch into it for better acceleration or to control the car. The switch, which worked a solenoid fitted to the gearbox's rear oil pump, became an established feature on automatic Jaguars.

Outwardly, it was easy to distinguish a Mark VIII Jaguar from the Mark VIIs. The updated saloon had two-tone paintwork with a distinctive chrome strip separating the top body colour from the bottom. This flowing line ran into cutaway rear-wheel spats. A larger, bolder radiator grille was fitted, as was a one-piece, rather than a split, windscreen. The interior was basically the same as that of the Mark VII, although there were some detail changes. One of the most noticeable was a remodelling of the rear seat to suggest two bucket seats with a substantial folding armrest in the centre. Rear-seat passengers were also provided with let-down walnut veneer picnic tables in the backs of the front seats. The bench seat fitted to automatic cars also contained a central pocket and an electric clock was recessed in the back facing the rear seats. Ashtrays and cigar lighters were let into the doors and the

The disc front brake and power-steering assembly on a right-hand-drive Mark IX Jaguar. Some left-hand-drive Mark VIII saloons had a similar steering arrangement.

thickness of the Dunlopillo rubber seat cushioning was increased. The luggage boot was also fully lined in Hardura material. These extra luxury trappings raised the car's overall weight by 1 cwt, but the extra performance provided by the B-type head more than made up for that.

The rear compartment of a Mark IX Jaguar which has been fitted with front seat belts. Although surface marks on the rear seat confirm its years of usage, the interior of this car looks to have been remarkably well preserved.

The rear section of a Mark IX limousine showing the neat installation of the radio receiver and the heater control below it in comfortable reach of the passengers. A wealth of wood veneer frames the glass panels of the division.

Few changes were made to the Mark VIII during its short production run. The camshafts were drilled for quieter cold starting early in 1957, and first rubber, then nylon, inserts were used between the rear spring leaves for smoother operation. The material for the radiator casting was changed from brass to alloy in July 1957 to save money, but, years later, proved to be prone to corrosion.

Power steering — long established as a feature on American cars — was fitted to some left-hand-drive Mark VIIIs from April 1958.

Front three-quarter view of the Mark IX Jaguar showing the clearly defined break line of the two-colour paint finish emphasized by chromed mouldings.

This used a pump driven from the back of the dynamo shaft to produce the hydraulic pressure to reduce the effort needed to turn the steering wheel. Jaguar opted for a substantial degree of assistance, making the steering very light to please the American market, which had long been used to featherlight steering. However, it is impossible to please all of the people all of the time, and many Europeans certainly were not pleased with this application of power-assisted steering. The extreme lightness removed much of the feel from the steering, although with prolonged use, and after sufficient confidence had been engendered by the Jaguar's excellent handling and stability, one became used to the feeling of insulation from the front wheels. The lightness of the steering was made less apparent than it might have been, however, by reducing the number of turns to 3.5 from lock to lock.

One of the minor changes made to the Mark VIII was the offer of optional Reutter adjustable-rake seats from July 1958. Production continued until December 1959, alongside a new model, the Mark IX, which was introduced in October 1958. This was because the Mark IX was virtually the same as the Mark VIII except that it had a new 3.8-litre version of the XK engine, power-assisted steering as standard, and disc brakes all round in common with the XK 140 sports car's successor, the XK 150, which had been introduced in 1957.

The 3.4-litre XK engine had been frequently bored out to 3.8 litres for competition, but the process was risky, often leading to cracking between the bores. When the bored-out 3.8-litre engines were running well, however, they showed a substantial increase in power and torque at little extra cost in fuel consumption. Therefore, Jaguars decided to design a new cylinder-block to accept that capacity. This new block, with bores of 87 mm rather than the 83 mm of the 3.4-litre unit, gave a capacity of 3,781 cc. Dry liners were used with the bores of the front three and the rear three being interconnected. Water passages ran between the two halves and the B-type cylinder-head was used.

The new engine produced an extra 30 bhp to give 220 bhp at 5,500 rpm, but, more important, it had a torque reading of 240 lb ft against 203 lb ft for the 3.4-litre with B-type head. This endowed the Mark IX with far greater performance, which was becoming necessary to keep it ahead of the large American cars which were receiving ever larger engines. The extra performance — with a maximum speed of nearly 115 mph — was kept under control by the use of disc brakes all round. These were of the latest Dunlop pattern, with quick-change pads like those of the XK 150, except that the discs were thicker because of the Mark IX's greater weight. A Lockheed vacuum servo was fitted with a reservoir to provide continued assistance in the event of the engine cutting-out.

These changes — with other details — made the Mark IX the ultimate development of the large early classic Jaguar saloons. Few changes were made during production, which went on until late in 1961. The heating unit had been uprated for the start of Mark IX production with a single 12-volt battery in place of the earlier twin six-volt units. Soon after, larger ball-joints were fitted to the front suspension to give a better range of movement. An electric tachometer was fitted midway through 1959 and an improved water pump was used from early-1960. At the same time a warning light indicating that the brake fluid was dangerously low, or that the handbrake had been left on, was fitted to the dashboard. The handbrake also received a stronger cable to reduce the possibility of stretching. Virtually the last changes were further improvements to the heater's capacity and larger rear lights in 1961 before the sensational new all-independently sprung Mark X took over in October 1961.

CHAPTER 3

The Mark 1 and 2

1955 to 1967

With the Mark VII saloon and the XK sports cars, Jaguar dominated two sectors of the high-performance car market in the early-1950s, and they needed only a medium-sized saloon along the same lines to take an even larger share. The resultant design was to be one of Jaguar's most successful cars, the Mark 1 of 1955, which was subsequently updated to the Mark 2 in 1959 and revised as the 240/340 in 1967, continuing in production until 1969 — a very long run by modern standards. The Mark 2 also formed the basis of the S-type saloons and their later developments, plus the small Daimlers made from 1962, which are covered in later chapters. These four/five-seater cars offered such an attractive combination of high performance and quality and they cost relatively so little that they rapidly established themselves as the definitive Jaguar saloon.

The first of these models was designed with a strong emphasis on economy. It had a 2.4-litre version of the XK engine, its capacity of 2,483 cc being achieved by shortening the stroke to 76.5 mm from 106 mm and retaining the existing 3.4-litre bore dimension of 83 mm. As a result, the engine was 3 inches shorter in overall height and weighed 50 lb less than the original XK unit. Normally it was fitted with an A-type cylinder-head with the softer 0.3125-inch-lift camshafts and twin Solex carburettors because economy was the prevailing theme, although in view of its short stroke, it could be revved harder than the 3.4-litre. In this form it produced 112 bhp at 5,750 rpm with 140 lb ft of torque at the low figure of 2,000 rpm. This meant that although the engine was well down on power compared with the 3.4-litre unit, it pulled very well at low revs, despite the shorter stroke, and this went a long way to compensate for the handicap of

reduced power.

The bodyshell broke new ground for Jaguar in that it was of unitary construction, eliminating the need for a separate chassis, a form of construction which was becoming increasingly popular in the early-1950s. It had the advantage of providing a far stiffer base on which to attach the car's running gear, notably the engine, gearbox and suspension, as well as its interior equipment; it was also lighter than the traditional method of construction involving a separate chassis and body.

Great attention was paid to making this structure really strong and because the car industry's knowledge of stress engineering was in its infancy in those days it tended to be too heavy in parts. If there was any chance that a mounting or a panel might be overstressed by components being attached to it, or that it might not be sufficiently rigid, it was made particularly strong (and heavy) — hence the very thick screen and rear pillars which supported the roof on the Mark 1. To ensure that there was adequate rigidity in the roof area, sunroofs were never fitted as standard to the Mark 1 or Mark 2, although, as it turned out, the shells were so strong in this area that it was quite safe to fit one. The lack of a sunroof, a standard item on the Mark VII, VIII and IX, also saved Jaguar money and, initially, economy of price as well as function was of paramount importance in the planning of the smaller car. Much attention was also paid to soundproofing the shell because such body units frequently acted as what amounted to a large drum. For this reason, everything that might transmit noise or vibration was attached to the bodyshell by rubber blocks.

The shell itself still retained some semblance of the traditional

The definitive body shape of the Mark 1 Jaguar had already been reached on this mock-up shell, but the details still had to be worked out. No bonnet line was visible because the possibility of the whole front-end hinging forward in a manner similar to that on the C-type and D-type sports-racing cars was under consideration. The radiator grille shape had yet to be finalized (although the influence of the XK sports cars was already evident) and various lighting arrangements were still under review.

This prototype Mark 1 is nearly complete, awaiting only final lighting decisions. No mascot had been fitted, indicating that this might have been the forerunner of the rare standard model.

Above, a pre-production Mark 1 saloon ready for testing, with prewar SS Jaguars and a Rover in the background. Note that only one overrider has been fitted at the back, pending a decision as to whether or not they should be left off the standard model in order to save cost. Left, the car is seen undergoing a form of baptism at the Motor Industry Research Association's test track near Nuneaton, a few miles from the Jaguar factory. The sidelights still had to be finalized on this car.

chassis layout in that it had two perimeter channel-sections running from the front of the car to the rear wheelarch, the steel floor and various transverse members being welded to them to form a rigid platform. The scuttle and rear seat pan were then welded to the platform for additional rigidity with two more box-members forming the sides of the engine bay. The hefty screen and rear pillars ran up to the roof, which formed the permanently-attached lid on the box. The outer body was built up around this

formation and welded to inner and outer wings and sills to further stiffen the structure.

The front suspension was similar to that of the Mark VII Jaguar except that it used coil springs rather than torsion bars because the design engineers anticipated difficulties in anchoring the torsion bar ends in the unitary chassis. The coil springs were attached to the lower wishbones and housed at their top ends in steel turrets, which were also the mounting points for the top

An early Special Equipment 2.4-litre Mark 1 showing its narrow radiator grille, somewhat reminiscent of that of the XK 140 introduced a year earlier.

Rear view of a Special Equipment Mark 1 showing the eventual design of its lighting, the position of the exhaust tailpipe and the use of chrome body trim.

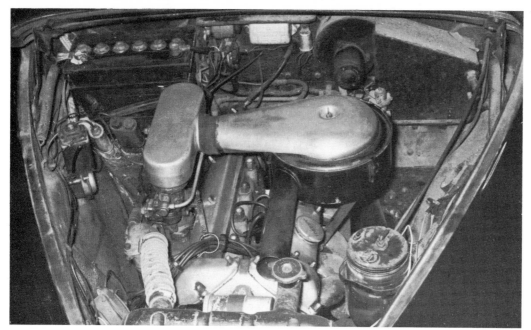

The installation of the 2.4-litre engine in a Mark 1 Jaguar saloon which has survived more than two decades of use in remarkably sound condition.

wishbones. The coil springs surrounded tubular shock absorbers and were connected at their bottom ends to an anti-roll bar.

The steel turrets were linked by a sturdy cross-member to form a subframe with two legs projecting forward to provide a wider mounting base. The Burman recirculating-ball steering gear was also mounted on this subframe, which was attached to the body unit by rubber blocks to insulate the shell from road noise and shock. Two universal joints were incorporated in the steering column to allow for movement in the subframe and, by coincidence, they enabled the steering column to fold up in the event of a severe frontal impact. Such safety features were sometimes designed into a car accidentally in those days! The subframe fitted underneath the engine and had to be removed before the sump could be dropped, but this proved to be a fairly easy job. The mountings were a great success in insulating the occupants of the car from noise and vibration.

The rear suspension did not feature a subframe, but it had rubber insulation for similar reasons. It used conventional half-elliptic springs in a most unconventional way. They were turned upside-down and one half was clamped to the bodyshell, leaving the other half projecting across the wheelarch to be attached to the axle at its extremity — making what in effect was a quarter-elliptic spring! The reason for this novel layout was that the engineers did not have confidence in the shell being strong enough to accept a conventionally mounted half-elliptic spring with shackles at the front and rear. Thus all the stresses were concentrated on the front end of the spring, which was secured via a central bolt with rubber insulation above and below the spring and at the front of the spring, allowing some longitudinal movement. The solid rear axle casing was further located by two trailing-arms running from the area of the seat pan to brackets above the axle. These located the axle in such a way that the application of power tended to turn it, so that the wheels were driven into the road. An adjustable Panhard rod stopped the axle

Close-up of the rear suspension showing one of the leaf springs and shock absorbers. The Panhard rod, painted white, can be seen running across to the right of the picture. One of the top links, painted black, can just be seen above it, next to the shock absorber. This picture was taken of a Mark 2 saloon, but the arrangements were very similar on the Mark 1.

The front suspension of a left-hand-drive Mark 1 Jaguar seen from the front of the jig on which the running gear was mounted before the body was dropped on top of it for final assembly. The universally-jointed steering column rests on the engine at this point, but it followed a more direct line when connected to the top half of its assembly in the bodyshell.

moving sideways. Rubber-mounted Girling telescopic shock absorbers were located at the top of the wheelarches. Lockheed brakes were fitted all round with a drum diameter of 11.125 inches and 15-inch wheels with 4.5-inch rims were provided.

Almost everything about the new Mark 1 was smaller than that of the Mark VII; the wheelbase was 8 ft 11.375 in, the length 15 ft 0.75 in, the width 5 ft 6.75 in, the height 4 ft 9.5 in, the front track 4 ft 6.625 in and the rear track rather narrow at 4 ft 2.125 in. This was to enable the rear wheels to be fitted behind spats in the tapering streamlined shape of the shell. This was frequently criticized for provoking alleged instability in the car at high speeds, although its weight distribution of 55 per cent front and 45 per cent rear from a total of 27 cwt probably had more to do with that.

None of the contemporary road tests found conclusive evidence to back up the rumours of instability, however. *The Motor* was the most constructive in its assessment of the Mark 1's rear suspension and concluded by giving some clue as to why it faced criticism. The magazine reported in July 1956:

'At a cursory glance the continuance of a rigid rear axle in the

The dashboard of a 2.4-litre Mark 1 automatic saloon, showing its central gearlever quadrant. The radio that has been fitted is a typical example of the period.

The dashboard of the manual Mark 1 saloon showing the position of the overdrive switch, which is just visible on the top rail at the right, partly concealed by the steering wheel rim.

Jaguar might appear to be flying in the face of progress, although the light construction of the axle, its cantilever springs, radius arms and Panhard rod promise something better than the conventional leaf-spring design. A very short distance on the road, particularly a secondary Continental road, vindicates the system completely, both as to riding comfort and as to roadholding power. On indifferent pavé, passengers may ride at any speed in comfort equivalent to that given by cars tested by *The Motor* with independent rear suspension. The real achievement of this suspension is that it combines such suppleness with damping, which quickly gets rid of the effects of hump-backs or trenches, and allows the car to roll slightly, but not wallow, in a fast corner.

'Tyre pressures play a considerable part in very controllable handling characteristics. The extra two pounds recommended for continuous cruising at 85 mph, or more, have little or no effect upon comfort, but are valuable at all speeds in making the steering light and sensitive. A quite false impression is gained from reference to the figure of 4½ turns between locks, for the turning circle is small (35 ft), the ratio progressive and the steering just neutral between under- and oversteering. As a result of this desirable balance, inherently good cornering can be improved by mildly skilful work on the accelerator pedal. As more of these cars come on the road, it is pertinent to explain that when the Jaguar is being cornered in a really enterprising manner the rear wheels, as seen from a following vehicle, present a rather

Interior of an early 2.4-litre Mark 1 automatic saloon. The outer portions of the dashboard were transposed when left-hand-drive was specified, as in this model, but curiously items such as the cigar lighter, fitted at the extreme right of the centre section, stayed in their original positions, making them rather awkward for drivers to reach.

The Mark 1 assembly line at Brown's Lane, with bodyshells waiting to be dropped on to the running gear jigs and XK 140 sports cars and Mark VIIM saloons on their own lines. Previously, Mark VII saloons and XK sports cars had shared the same lines.

alarming spectacle, of which no trace is felt from the driving seat. The car has no vices and feels equally safe and controllable on a slippery road.'

Although the Mark 1 was less powerful than the Mark VII, it weighed only three quarters as much as the big saloon and had a smaller frontal area, so it proved slightly faster on acceleration and could provide 100 mph with 25 mpg. Furthermore, it cost only about 80 per cent of the price of the contemporary Mark VIIM.

The interior was trimmed to a similar standard to that of the Mark VIIM and was only slightly smaller, the difference being mainly noticeable in the back. In fact, the headroom was virtually the same as that of the much higher Mark VIIM because the body

did not have to be built on top of the chassis. The driver and passengers had to adopt a new technique for entry, however, stepping in and down over high sills rather than up and across a flat floor as in the case of the Mark VIIM. A slightly cheaper Standard model Mark 1 was listed, but few were built, as the small saving in price meant the deletion of many accepted Jaguar features fitted to the Special Equipment model, such as a rev counter, rear armrest, screen washers, foglamps, cigar lighter and heater. A popular optional extra in Europe was a Laycock de Normanville overdrive working on top gear only, which was linked to a 4.55:1-ratio Salisbury hypoid-bevel rear axle. Normally a 4.27:1 axle would be fitted, but the overdrive gave a relaxed top ratio of 3.54:1 while engaged.

Outwardly, the new Mark 1 was as stunning as any other Jaguar had been with a frontal treatment very much like that of the contemporary XK 140 sports car. Its profile was completely new, however, with smooth lines accentuated by the use of full spats on the rear wheels. The rearward treatment, particularly around the back window, was reminiscent of earlier Jaguars, particularly the Mark VII, while the slim tail was more like that of an XK sports car.

There was so much that was new about the Mark 1 that some teething troubles were almost inevitable, although to give credit to Jaguar, they were relatively few. The Panhard rod mounting had to be reinforced from May 1956, and even then it could prove fragile and it remained the Achilles heel of hard-driven Mark 1 and Mark 2 cars. The dampers were uprated and in June 1956 a crankshaft damper was fitted to the 2.4-litre engine. Its alloy sump was replaced by a cheaper steel one in November 1956, the carburettor settings were improved and overdrive cars received a 4.27:1 rear axle ratio as standard. Various factory modifications

The revised frontal treatment of the late-model 2.4-litre Mark 1 saloon showing its 3.4-litre-style wider radiator grille.

Side profile of the 3.4-litre Mark 1 showing the line of its cutaway rear-wheel spats.

Wire wheels were popular and effective options on the Mark 1 saloon. This car's disc brakes can be seen through the wheels, which are the early-pattern 60-spoke version.

were marketed for the 2.4-litre engine to improve its performance. Stage One involved carburettor changes and a straight-through silencer, which gave 119 bhp; Stage Two gave the addition of high-lift camshafts, a new distributor and 131 bhp; and Stage Three, with the B-type head, 1.75-inch SU carburettors, a new distributor and dual exhaust gave 150 bhp. Stage Three also entailed the fitting of a stronger clutch, and because the cylinder-head was not available on exchange it took the cost of a 2.4-litre Mark 1 up to close to that of a Mark VIIM or Mark VIII. Close-ratio gears, stiffer dampers and a high-ratio steering box could also be fitted, the latter giving four turns from lock to lock.

Despite the availability of this tuning equipment, the 2.4-litre was not a great success in the United States. The saving in fuel mattered so little that absolute performance was more important, particularly as the standard 2.4-litre was fairly expensive for an economy car and only 20 per cent cheaper than the larger Mark VIIM or Mark VIII, which offered a similar performance with

The Mark 2 Jaguar was a great improvement over the Mark 1, its appearance being enhanced by many subtle detail changes.

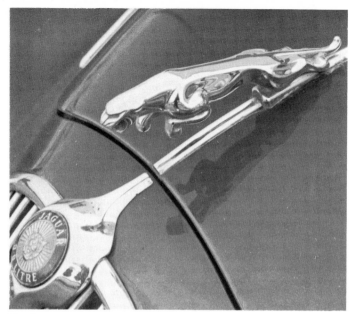

The famous leaping Jaguar mascot as fitted to nearly all the saloon cars covered in this book.

which had just been introduced. Apart from that, the car was little changed outwardly other than by the fitment of new cutaway spats to help brake cooling and the deletion of the built-in foglights. With 190 bhp available the Mark 1's performance was transformed to a maximum speed of 120 mph and a 0-60 mph time of 9 seconds. Jaguar were far ahead of their rivals once more and the 3.4-litre Mark 1 immediately became a best-seller especially as its price was still less than that of the big saloon.

Such performance presented its problems, however, particularly when it came to stopping the 28.5-cwt car (which had 58 per cent of its weight concentrated over the front wheels). Optional wire wheels helped the brake cooling, but they did not allow enough heat to disperse, nor did they suck in any cooling air, so severe brake fade could be easily induced on hard-driven cars and Jaguar hurriedly introduced the option of the XK 150's disc brakes all round for both 2.4-litre and 3.4-litre Mark 1s from late-1957. These were such an improvement that few cars were

The power unit of the 3.8-litre Mark 2 Jaguar. This car has been fitted with a Kenlowe electric fan, the thermostat switch for which can be seen in the right front corner of the bonnet opening, next to the radiator header tank.

the option of an automatic gearchange. The Americans wanted, quite simply, a 3.4-litre Mark 1, which is what they were offered in March 1957. The car was actually announced in February 1957, but the factory suffered a severe fire and this delayed production.

The new Mark 1 had to be extensively modified to take the 190-bhp 3.4-litre engine with its SU carburettors, B-type head and twin exhausts from the Mark VIII. It had a 10-inch, rather than a 9-inch, clutch with the manual gearbox and the option of the Borg-Warner automatic transmission. A new rear axle was made up from the heavier Mark VIII centre-section with 2.4-litre ends and the 3.54:1 ratio was standard, with a 3.77:1 ratio being fitted on overdrive cars. The Panhard rod mounting was modified to suit the new axle.

A larger radiator was also fitted, which entailed the use of a wider grille, very much like that of the new XK 150 sports car,

A 3.8-litre Mark 2 pictured on test by the prestigious British magazine *Motor Sport,* which proclaimed it to be one of the world's best saloon cars. 'That such a car can be sold for just over £1,800 is a commercial miracle understood only by Sir William Lyons,' said editor William Boddy.

Two doors have been removed from this left-hand-drive manual-transmission Mark 2 show model to reveal the interior to its best advantage. The front seats have been reclined to their fullest extent.

Close-up of the driving compartment of a right-hand-drive Jaguar Mark 2 with manual gearbox.

made with drum brakes after that. With full equipment, the 3.4-litre Mark 1 became almost as fast as the XK 150 because its unitary construction kept its weight down to little more than 1 cwt above that of the sports car, which still had a chassis based on the Mark V.

Costs were reduced by some measure of standardization in the Mark 1's bodyshell, with the 2.4-litre and the 3.4-litre both receiving the same wide-grille frontal treatment and cutaway spats from September 1957. Such was the power and the torque of the 3.4-litre engine, it was possible to wag the tail away from a standing start, especially in the wet, so a Thornton Powr-Lok limited-slip differential was made an option from the summer of 1958; this proved beneficial to saloon car racing drivers, who were already dominating touring car events with their Mark 1s. Dampers were improved and 'quick-change' disc pads were introduced from January 1959.

The optional wire wheels, which were of 5-inch rim width, were uprated from 60 to 72 spokes as demand for them increased; Dunlop had originally started making 60-spoke wire wheels for lighter sports cars and it was not until they were adopted for the heavier Jaguar saloons that the necessity for stronger wheels became apparent. Other modifications in keeping with those on the Mark IX and XK 150 ranges were made in 1959, including fitting a half-inch fan belt and pulley, lead-indium crankshaft

57

bearings, larger diameter front suspension ball-joints and an electric rev counter, before the much modified Mark 2 was introduced in October 1959.

This was to be the most successful classic Jaguar saloon ever, a superb revision of the Mark 1 which retained everything that was good about the original and improved on most of the weak points. The two most apparent changes were the redesigned windows, to give more glass area, and the much wider rear axle. The windows had been revised when it became apparent that the roof support pillars did not need to be so thick. The windscreen was made an inch deeper, and new door pressings gave between 1.25 inches and 1.5 inches more glass depth and a total of 9.5 inches of extra width. The rear window was made 3 inches deeper and 7 inches wider, practically meeting the rear quarter-lights as it wrapped round. The car's appearance was also changed substantially by a 3.5-inch increase in the rear track width, which was really

The dashboard and controls of the Mark 2 manual model with a standard radio installation. From the left, the switches in the centre panel are for interior lights, panel lights, interior fan, ignition (by key), cigar lighter, starter (by button), map light, windscreen wipers and electric washers. The centre switch above the cigar lighter controls the sidelights, headlights and foglights.

The luggage compartment of the Mark 2 Jaguar with its jack clipped in place on the rear bulkhead. The tiny badge on the centre of the bumper bar carries a warning triangle and reads 'Disc brakes'. Such signs, popular additions to the backs of many cars with exceptional stopping power in the late-1950s and early-1960s, were a standard fitting on the Mark 2.

intended to improve stability, of course. The rear suspension remained the same, but the front suspension's geometry was rearranged to raise the car's roll-centre. The combination of a wider rear track and the front suspension modifications made the Mark 2 a much more manageable car. Other detail changes were made with a slightly different radiator grille, built-in spotlamps and sidelamps on top of the wings. The rear valance was also made deeper to cover the fuel tank.

The Mark 2 was offered with three engine capacities, 2.4 litres, 3.4 litres and 3.8 litres, all units using the B-type head. This improved power on the 2.4-litre to 120 bhp with 144 lb ft of torque, the 3.4-litre produced 210 bhp and 216 lb ft and the 3.8 litre 220 bhp and 240 lb ft. Otherwise, the 2.4-litre unit was the same as that fitted to the Mark 1. The 3.8-litre engine was like that of the Mark IX saloon and was one of the options in the XK 150 sports car. However, the Mark 2 did not receive the 265 bhp straight-port head, triple-carburettor 3.8-litre engine fitted to the most potent of the XKs, the XK 150S. This was because the carburettors took up too much space under the bonnet and would have needed extensive sheet-metal alterations to accommodate their extra length and width on the inlet side.

However, most customers were of the opinion that the 3.8-litre Mark 2 had enough power and torque anyway, sufficient to give them 125 mph with a 0-60 mph time of 8.5 seconds. A Powr-Lok limited-slip differential was fitted as standard to cope with the power and torque, but it remained an optional extra for the 2.4-litre and 3.4-litre cars. Power-assisted steering similar to that fitted to the Mark IX saloon was also available as an option, although only from October 1960 on the home market. This power steering came in for some criticism, particularly from European countries, for being too light, especially as Jaguar retained a new lower-geared steering, which had been fitted to the

Mark 2 cars to cope with the extra weight over the front wheels.

The Mark 2 had a completely new interior that was to form the pattern for such designs in Jaguars for years to come. The main instruments, the speedometer and the rev counter, were moved to a position in front of the driver from their traditional home in the centre of the dashboard. The ammeter, fuel, oil-pressure and water-temperature gauges were mounted in the centre of the facia above a long line of toggle switches working such items as the windscreen wipers, electric washers, plus the ignition and starter controls. This centre panel hinged down for access to the wiring loom. The overdrive switch or automatic gearchange control was mounted in a binnacle above the steering column. A brake fluid warning light and a warning for the handbrake — which was mounted on the floor beside the driver — were also provided on the dashboard. The seats were redesigned with deeper squabs and wider cushions, and a radio could be fitted in the deep centre console. Otherwise, the interior followed traditionally plush Jaguar lines. The heater was made more powerful, but it

An export-specification Mark 2 Jaguar equipped with the popular option of 72-spoke wire wheels and whitewall tyres.

Many extras were available for the Mark 2 saloon, and this example has been equipped with wing mirrors and a radiator muff.

remained inferior to those fitted to most American cars.

Only 3.8-litre models were exported to America and most of those had wire wheels in common with many cars sent to other countries. This was because the Mark 2 was, quite rightly, considered to be an exclusive sports saloon that cost a little more than average. Therefore, the people who bought them wanted the ultimate in performance and were willing to pay for the privilege, hence the 3.8-litre engine, wire wheels and all the goodies. There were just two points on which the Americans compromised when it came to ultimate performance. They generally liked power steering and an automatic gearbox, as with their domestic cars, so the manual 3.8-litre with unassisted steering did not sell so well in the United States. Home-produced air-conditioning units were also fitted to American Jaguars fairly frequently.

Numerous detail improvements were made to the Mark 2 range during its production life, but little that was of major significance apart from a change of gearbox in 1965 and the restyling as the 240/340 in 1967. The 2.4-litre and the 3.4-litre engines remained substantially unchanged, but a number of detail modifications were made to the 3.8-litre unit to combat rather high oil consumption. These included fitting a modified crankshaft rear cover for improved sump sealing in January 1960. Stiffer shock absorbers were fitted soon after and an oil-pressure gauge with revised readings from March 1960. This was because the original gauge showed the normal top pressure of 60 psi only about halfway up its travel, with the normal running pressure of 40/45 psi apparently dangerously low on the scale. Recalibration to move the 40 psi mark nearer the middle of the scale put a lot of owners' minds at ease.

Despite the pressure of introducing the sensational new E-type sports car, Jaguars found time to continually update the fittings in the Mark 2 range, as could be seen by a new telescopic rear-view mirror in April 1960. In keeping with the 3.4-litre and 3.8-litre engines in other Jaguars which used SU carburettors, the old oil-bath air filter was replaced with a modern paper-element fitting and the engine breathers were rerouted into the carburettors; that was one of the first requirements of the Californian clean-air campaign.

The indicator switch and overdrive stalk (if fitted) were reversed to more conventional left and right-hand positions from June 1960, and the heater was modified soon after. This was to prevent unwanted hot air entering the interior! Wider steel wheels, with 5-inch rims rather than 4.5-inch, were fitted from September 1960. Further detail changes took place in November that year when an organ-type accelerator pedal was fitted and the steering column was lowered to allow more room for adjustment. Minor modifications were made to the interior, including strengthening the side window frames. A new SU fuel pump was fitted and the power steering pump improved. These changes accompanied the more visual one of the replacement of the old glass brake fluid container with a plastic type.

A modified crankshaft rear cover was fitted to XK engines from January 1961 in an attempt to improve sump sealing when the car was parked facing uphill with the engine switched off.

Handling was further improved on all cars by the standardization of a stiffer anti-roll bar, which had previously been an option. More rigid forged wishbones replaced the

Just before the 240/340 range was announced, British Leyland economized on the Mark 2 Jaguar by deleting the foglights and substituting horn grilles, besides changing to Ambla upholstery.

Frontal view of the Jaguar 240, showing its slim-line bumper.

pressed-steel items in February 1960. Underbonnet checks were made easier by fitting a tubular guide for the engine oil dipstick, and the lubrication system was improved by fitting a larger oil pump in June 1961, which needed a new sump to go with it.

Cars with disc brakes have often been criticised for having weak handbrakes, particularly when the pads or linkage become worn. This is because the disc pads do not have the same binding effect as some of the lining systems fitted to drum brakes, and it is difficult to exert sufficient leverage on them by manual means. Jaguar improved the handbrake in August 1961 by fitting a self-adjusting mechanism and water deflectors were fitted for the front hubs.

The battle against oil leaks continued in December 1961 with the fitting of a new crankshaft rear oil seal incorporating asbestos rope. Larger diameter and more durable propeller-shaft universal-joints were fitted at the same time. Cars built from January 1962 could be readily identified by seat-belt mounting points welded into the shell. From February that year it was possible to have a high-output dynamo fitted as an option; this was standardized in October 1963 and many of the cars built between those dates were police vehicles, which had a lot of extra electrical equipment. Drilled camshafts were fitted to all engines for quieter starting from May 1962.

The oil consumption of the 3.8-litre engine was dramatically reduced from September 1962 when Brico Maxiflex scraper rings were fitted to the pistons. Sealed-beam headlamps were also fitted to right-hand-drive cars at this time. The Panhard rod mounting bracket to the body was made even stronger from January 1963 to counter the inherent weakness there, and inside the car, rear-seat legroom, which could be really restricted when the front seats were right back, was improved by cutting away the bottoms of the seats to allow the rear seat passengers' feet to slip beneath them. Problems with overheating in some Mark 2s were countered by fitting a 9 psi pressure cap to the radiator in March 1963. More durable dampers were fitted at the same time and the side window frames were strengthened from the following month.

Further experimentation with the cooling problem — caused chiefly by lack of maintenance in hot climates — resulted in a 7 psi radiator cap being used from September 1963, with an improved water pump. Sealed-for-life propeller-shaft universal-joints were fitted at the same time as part of a campaign to reduce

maintenance on the Mark 2. Finally, the centre button on the steering column was made to work in conjunction with the horn ring from October 1963.

A further assault on the oil consumption problem began in January 1964 when a revised sump with a new oil pump was fitted to all Mark 2s, followed by modified pistons on the 3.8-litre that allowed an easier return passage to the sump for oil picked up by the control rings. Attempts were made to improve lubrication of the front suspension at the same time. This involved nylon washers in the top and bottom wheel swivel and tie-rod seals. The idea was that an excess of grease could escape via the nylon washer rather than by damaging the seals, but this did not always happen in practice as sometimes a small obstruction in the grease passage could force the lubricant back through its entry nipple without ever having reached the bearing. Grease nipples were also fitted to the front wheel bearings on steel-wheeled cars to save having to take the bearings to pieces to lubricate them.

The cooling system was still the subject of development, with a 4 psi radiator cap being fitted from May 1964, and a new SU fuel

Rear detail of the 240, showing its revised bumper bar and overriders, with the twin exhaust system.

The 240's engine, showing the new ribbed camshaft covers, which were finished in black and polished aluminium.

pump — shared with the S-type saloons, which had been introduced at the end of 1963 — was used on the Mark 2 from May.

Detail modifications were made to the automatic gearbox and torque converter in June 1965 to improve the gearchange before the major change in the manual transmission in July. This involved fitting the all-synchromesh four-speed gearbox that had been used on other Jaguar saloons from December in the previous year and on the E-type sports car from September. This gearbox was a great success, providing a light and easy change by virtue of Warner inertia-lock baulk-ring synchromesh on all gears, whereas the old gearbox, with synchromesh on only the top three ratios, was very strong, but could be obstructive. The new gearbox still suffered from the old fault of needing long movements for the gearlever, although they were a little shorter than with the previous version. A new starter motor and diaphragm clutch were fitted at the same time, with a self-adjusting slave cylinder for the clutch. This made the clutch lighter to operate and compensated for normal wear in the linings. Together, these two features — the lighter and easier gearchange and clutch action — made more difference to the Mark 2 than any other modification during its production run.

Still further development of the cooling system resulted in a new radiator and fan cowling in December 1965. Then came the next big change in the 'feel' of a Mark 2 and it was not for the better; in an attempt to keep down its cost, Ambla plastic upholstery was used, with the traditional Jaguar leather becoming an option at extra cost from September 1966.

Nearly a year later, in July 1967, Marles Varamatic power-assisted steering gear replaced the previous system where specified. This new power steering felt much better, with the overall ratio varying from 4.25 turns from lock to lock in the straight-ahead position to half that by half-lock. In this way more power and movement was exerted initially, with more resistance and 'feel' becoming evident as the steering wheel was turned.

Two months later, in September 1967, the Mark 2 was revised in the form of a new saloon, with a choice of 2.4-litre or 3.4-litre engine and called the 240 or 340. The 3.8-litre option was dropped as by then variants of the S-type saloon had been introduced with a 4.2-litre version of the XK engine. The 240 and 340 were identical apart from the engine and badges and the option of power steering on the 340 only. The chief difference in appearance from the previous Mark 2 was the substitution of slimmer bumpers, similar to those of other contemporary Jaguar saloons, which meant that the valances below the bumpers had to be revised. In addition, to save money, the built-in foglamps were replaced with grilles like those of the early Mark 1 saloons. The theme of the 240 and 340 was cost-cutting wherever possible, and in this there was considerable success because they cost only about the same as the original Mark 1 had 12 years earlier, and in that time the value of money had decreased by half! At the same time, more power was extracted from the 2.4-litre engine by fitting it with a straight-port cylinder-head like that of the 4.2-litre engines, twin SU carburettors and a dual exhaust system. In this form, the 2.4-litre unit produced 133 bhp and 146 lb ft of torque,

The Jaguar 340 pictured soon after it was launched amongst alternative forms of express transport.

which gave the car a higher top speed of 106 mph with a much better 0-60 mph time of 12.5 seconds against 17.3 for the 2.4-litre Mark 2. The 340's engine was the same as that in the 3.4-litre Mark 2, retaining its B-type cylinder-head. The only difference was that it shared new ribbed cam covers with the 240 unit, which were also used on other XK engines. Items such as a paper-element air filter for the 2.4-litre engine and side cable entries rather than top entries for the distributor were standardized. These cars also had the latest Borg-Warner Model 35 automatic gearbox where this form of transmission was specified. The 240 and 340 continued in production until they were replaced by the new XJ range.

CHAPTER 4

The Mark X, 420 G, S-type and 420

1961 to 1970

The voluptuous Mark X introduced in October 1961 was the first of a new generation of Jaguar saloons that was far more advanced technically than anything before them. The Mark X was a really big car by European standards, having been designed specifically for the American market; the smaller S-type saloons that were developed from it amounted to a combination of the best qualities of the medium-sized Mark 2 range and those of the Mark X; and the 420 and Daimler Sovereign developed from the S-types were simply updated versions of the earlier model. The distinguishing feature of these cars was that they had Jaguar's new independent rear suspension system, which had been introduced on the E-type sports car in March 1961.

This new suspension gave a more comfortable ride with excellent handling and proved to be capable of transmitting the XK engine's considerable power with the greatest of ease. It was exactly the same as that of the E-type in design, but considerably wider as the Mark X saloon was one of the widest cars ever made. The overall width of 6 ft 4 in made it the widest British car in production at the time, necessitating a rear track of 4 ft 10 in. The layout of the rear suspension was quite ingenious, using the drive-shafts as the top links in a wishbone configuration. A tubular wishbone ran beneath each drive-shaft and a radius-arm each side provided the other suspension links. Two dampers each side, one in front of the drive-shaft and one behind, were bolted to the lower wishbones and were surrounded by coil springs, with their top mountings on a subframe which contained the differential and inboard disc brakes. The drive-shafts, each of which had two universal-joints, were located in hub-carriers pivoted at one end of the wishbones with the wishbone's other pivots in the subframe

under the brakes. The subframe and radius-arms were attached to the bodyshell by rubber mountings, which effectively insulated the body from vibrations and noise. Internally, the differential was the same as that of the Mark 2 saloon, with Powr-Lok limited-slip clutches as standard.

Not only was the Mark X's body large, but it was very strong. It was based on two massive sills, 7 inches deep and 7 inches wide on their flat inner sections. The floor which connected them and contained the transmission tunnel was braced by substantial box-section pressings between the front bulkhead and the rear seat pan, which was also boxed-in. Substantial rear wheelarch assemblies ran back to the tail with the rear suspension subframe mounting arch and luggage boot floor linking them. Equally strong box-members ran forward at the front to take the engine and a beam for mounting the front suspension. Inner wings at the front and the passenger footwells contributed to the rigidity of the shell, which was so strong that the roof and its supporting pillars played a relatively minor role in its total rigidity. In a similar manner to that of the Mark 1 and Mark 2 saloons, the Mark X's outer body panels were welded on to the basic inner structure. The four doors were exceptionally wide, 3 ft 4.5 in at the front and 2 ft 7.5 in at the rear. Like the rest of the car, they were heavy, being mounted on substantial vertical box-section beams.

The body's lines had a decidedly futuristic look about them for 1961. Apart from being exceptionally wide, the Mark X was very long at 16 ft 10 in, although it retained the same 10-ft wheelbase as that of the Mark IX saloon which it replaced. It was much lower, however, at only 4 ft 6.75 in. The traditional Jaguar shape was preserved in the new, wider, radiator grille set off by a four-

The embryo Mark X Jaguar at an early mock-up stage before the lines and bumpers were refined to their eventual shape.

Jaguar test driver Fred Merrill puts a pre-production Mark X saloon through its paces in the Basque country near the Spanish border with France.

The Mark X as it went into production. This is a left-hand-drive car registered in Jersey.

The triple-carburettor 4.2-litre version of the XK engine as installed in a 420 G. The earlier 3.8-litre version of this engine was of similar appearance except that it had polished aluminium camshaft covers.

The front suspension mounting beam on the Mark X Jaguar.

headlamp system. New slim-line bumpers with a pronounced wrap-round, especially at the back, emphasized the width and the long, low look. The luggage boot, with its twin petrol tanks in the wings, was exceptionally large and the only problem presented by the styling was that the sills — so necessary for rigidity — were exceptionally deep and could hinder entry and exit for the elderly or infirm. The roofline and windows bore a distinct family resemblance to the other Jaguar saloons.

At the time the Mark X was being designed, Jaguar also had a new V-12 engine in mind — which was eventually introduced in the E-type sports car in 1971 — so the engine compartment was also very wide. However, the Mark X's performance, with its six-cylinder XK engine in its most powerful 265 bhp form, was still very impressive despite an unladen weight of around 2 tons. The actual performance figures of a maximum speed approaching 120 mph with a 0-60 mph time of approximately 12 seconds incurred a penalty, however, of fuel-consumption figures in the region of 14 mpg. The engine's high power output was achieved by using the E-type sports car's straight-port cylinder-head with triple SU carburettors and a twin exhaust system. The capacity was the same as that of the Mark IX saloon, 3,781 cc.

Two types of transmission were used, like those in the Mark IX and Mark 2 saloons: a Borg-Warner automatic gearbox or a four-speed manual with the option of overdrive. When the manual gearbox was fitted, a 10-inch Borg and Beck clutch was used.

The rear subframe was detachable as a unit, complete with the final drive, drive-shafts and suspension components. The front suspension was similar to that of the Mark 2 saloon, with top and bottom wishbones and one large coil spring either side, except that it was mounted on a simpler subframe, which took the form of a substantial beam with suspension pillars at either end. It was mounted in the same manner as the Mark X's rear subframe — to insulate the bodyshell from noise and vibration — and could be detached in a similar fashion. The front disc brakes were 10.75 inches in diameter, 0.75 inches larger than those at the rear. They were operated by a new servo similar to that used on the E-type sports car. It was made by Dunlop — who also provided the brakes — under licence from Kelsey-Hayes in the United States, using a bellows to exert mechanical pressure on the brake master cylinders rather than the more conventional pressure on the

The luggage boot interior of a Mark X Jaguar with vertical spare wheel mounting. Both the compartment and lid are fully trimmed.

Rear three-quarter view of the 420 G, a model that was identical in appearance from this angle to the Mark X, except for the chrome body line and luggage boot badge.

The cloth-upholstered rear seat of a Mark X limousine with its walnut-faced division. Oddly, this car does not have electrically controlled windows, although it has all manner of other fittings such as a flexible reading lamp extension above the rear quarter light and a cocktail cabinet.

diameter road wheels — 14 inches — were fitted to the Mark X in keeping with its space-age image. They had 5.5-inch-wide rims carrying 7.50—14 tyres, however, which were much wider than had been used before on a Jaguar saloon.

Jaguar took advantage of the fact that they were designing a completely new bodyshell to revise their much-criticized interior heating, installing a new system in the scuttle, based around a Marston heat exchanger. Air was admitted through an intake in

Close-up of the rear compartment of a Mark X Jaguar with its picnic tables folded. Note the deep bolstering of the seat cushion.

hydraulic lines. The chief advantage of using this servo was that it was independent of the hydraulic system and required little maintenance. A disadvantage, however, was that it did not always give a great deal of assistance because it was more susceptible than a normal servo to variations in engine vacuum pressure. Twin hydraulic circuits were used as a safety measure to give some braking if one circuit failed.

Power-assisted steering like that used on the Mark X's predecessor, the Mark IX saloon, was used with a ratio that gave 4.5 turns of the steering wheel from lock to lock. Unusually small-the scuttle to be piped to four outlets, two in the front of the car and two at the back. The front outlets could be adjusted to serve the occupants' feet or bodies; the others led down the transmission tunnel to play on the rear passengers' feet. This intake of air could be directed past the heat exchanger for ventilation only, or through the heater's matrix to give warm air. The intake was boosted by two large electric fans, with vacuum-servo assistance for the basic controls. Quarter-lights were provided in the front and rear windows for additional ventilation. This heating system worked reasonably well by contemporary standards, but suffered chiefly from the fact that the amount of warm air could not be adjusted; it was all or nothing. Also, the means of ventilating the interior was still primitive, and the whole heating and ventilation system was soon to be outdated by simpler developments on cheaper cars.

The interior was based on that of the Mark 2 with everything on a larger and grander scale. The instruments and switches were laid out in a similar fashion and were set in a vast expanse of walnut. The front seats were large, flat and individual, with reclining backrests and built-in picnic trays and vanity mirrors

behind. They were certainly comfortable, but they came in for criticism in that they did not give enough lateral support. Hard cornering, of which the Mark X was certainly capable, was likely to send the passengers sliding across the polished leather seats! Electric windows were offered as an option, with individual controls on each passenger door and further controls grouped beside the driver on the deep transmission console.

Throughout its production run, the Mark X benefitted from improvements made to the Mark 2 and E-type, such as the asbestos rope crankshaft rear seal fitted from January 1962. It also received individual modifications, such as improving the radiator from March 1963, following failures with the unit which had been specially designed for the Mark X. The heater controls were also altered at the same time so that the scuttle air intake could be opened separately. This meant that it could be kept shut until the heat exchanger had warmed-up, rather than opening immediately the 'warm' button was pressed and then letting in volumes of cold air if the car had only just been started. A heated rear window element was also fitted from April 1962 when sufficient supplies became available. It had been intended to fit this useful device

Sheer luxury. The interior of a Mark X automatic equipped with the optional electric window lifts.

Rear view of a Jaguar 3.8-litre S-type saloon showing its revised wings and new Mark X-style bumper, overriders, rear window and roofline.

A rolling chassis of an S-type Jaguar awaits dispatch to an Italian coachbuilder for a special body. The basic construction, with its integral fuel tanks and high-mounted fuel pumps, can be seen. The driver's seat, of course, is non-standard!

The car on the right, an S-type, is lined up beside a Mark 2 (centre) and a 240 (left) to show the family resemblance and to highlight the subtle differences in frontal treatment.

The Jaguar S-type equipped with optional wire wheels in left-hand-drive form. The car's Mark 2 ancestry can be clearly seen in this picture.

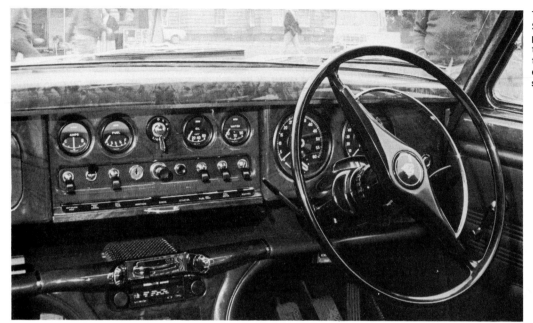

from the start of production, and provision had been made for it in the wiring loom.

Drilled camshafts for quieter starting were fitted to the Mark X's engine from May 1962, in common with those on the other Jaguars' XK engines, with Brico scraper rings being added from September 1962 to cut oil consumption.

Despite their relatively small size — dictated by the 14-inch road wheels — the brakes on the Mark X were reasonably adequate, but they took a hammering because of the car's weight. Their efficiency and durability was improved by fitting larger wheel cylinders from July 1962, then thicker discs in January 1963. Improved dampers were fitted to the Mark X in the same month to stop it wallowing along, and modifications were made to the rear subframe mountings, including using a better bonding agent. Special couplings were fitted to the electric windows to prevent their jamming wide open or closed. The Mark X's engine also received a new distributor, in common with the E-type, in April 1963.

Meanwhile, much development work had been going on to graft the new rear suspension into the Mark 2's shell. The result was the S-type saloons introduced in October 1963. The changes required to fit the independent rear suspension to the Mark 2 were far more extensive than at first might be imagined and resulted in a car that combined numerous elements of the Mark X with those of the Mark 2. Apart from the rear suspension, with a narrower track, the S-type had a redesigned tail — along Mark X lines — and a revised roofline that extended the maximum height of the roof further back and entailed fitting the rear window in a more upright position. The front of the car was restyled as well, although this exercise followed closely on the Mark 2's lines. Mark X-style slim-line bumpers were also fitted in keeping with the restyling.

The interior was also redesigned, far more along Mark X lines than those of the Mark 2, although there was still a strong family resemblance to the smaller car. The front seats, in particular, were like those of the Mark X, although they did a far better job of locating their occupants because they were narrower. They were also thinner, lacking the picnic tables fitted to the Mark X and Mark 2, which had the benefit of allowing more kneeroom in the back. Like the Mark X the S-type's seats reclined at the touch of a lever. The rear seats were made thinner, too, to give more legroom and reclined further back for the same reason; the revised roofline allowed this without loss of headroom. The dashboard and centre console were like those in the Mark X, and had a full-width parcel shelf, again like the Mark X.

Mechanically, the S-types were similar to the Mark 2s except that the 2.4-litre engine was not available. This was because they were 3 cwt heavier than the Mark 2, and it would not have given the new car a sufficiently brisk performance. The whole idea of the 3.4-litre and 3.8-litre S-types was to produce a car that was more manageable than the Mark X and more luxurious than the Mark 2, with a better ride because of the independent rear suspension.

In size, it was almost the same as the Mark 2 except that it was longer, at 15 ft 7 in against 15 ft 0.75 in, the extra length being taken up entirely by the new rear-end with its large luggage boot and twin petrol tanks like those on the Mark X. The fitting of the rear suspension — which had a wider track than the Mark 2 at 4 ft 6.25 in against 4 ft 5.375 in (partly because of wider, 5.5-inch, wheel rims) entailed extensive changes under the skin.

The box-section beams on which the Mark 2's cantilever springs were mounted were extended backwards over the wheelarches and under the luggage boot floor to the extreme rear of the car. The boot floor was reinforced and welded to the extended box-sections with an integral spare-wheel well for extra rigidity. The rear wheelarches were also welded into the structure for additional strengthening in a similar manner to those on the Mark X. Thus the S-types adopted the Mark X's built-in wheel fairings, rather than the detachable spats of the Mark 2. The rear suspension assembly, with its subframe, was identical to that of the E-type sports car and the Mark X saloon except for variations in track. The front suspension of the S-type was the same as that of the Mark 2, however, with its complex subframe. The steering was modified, though, when power assistance was specified, to give only 3.5 turns of the steering wheel from lock to lock, to counter criticisms of the ratios used on the Mark 2 and Mark X. In company with the Mark 2, only twin carburettors could be

fitted because of the restricted space available under the bonnet. The B-type cylinder-head was retained on both the 3.4-litre and 3.8-litre S-type engines, and the same manual, manual-with-overdrive, or automatic-transmission options were available. The overall gearing remained the same as that on the Mark 2.

The rear seat of an S-type saloon with the central armrest folded down to convert it into a comfortable two-seater.

This view of a Jaguar 420 emphasizes its close resemblance in styling to the larger 420 G.

The engine compartment of the Jaguar 420 showing the neat installation of the transversely mounted air cleaner with the oil dipstick visible beyond it.

than if they had been greased properly. The modified pistons fitted to the 3.8-litre engines were used on the Mark X and S-type from March 1964 and the 4 psi radiator cap on the S-type in company with the Mark 2 two months later.

The next major change, in October 1964, was confined at first to the Mark X and the E-type sports car. This was the introduction of a 4.2-litre version of the XK engine with the new all-synchromesh gearbox, which appeared later on the Mark 2 and from December that year as an option on the S-type. It was not introduced across the range at the same time because of initial shortages in supply. The engine's capacity increase, from 3,781 cc to 4,235 cc, was aimed at producing more torque to keep the Mark X abreast of huge American V-8-powered competitors. It was achieved by using larger, 92.07 mm, bores in a modified cylinder-block. The extra space for their liners was found by staggering the bores with the first and last cylinders moving outwards slightly and the centre two moving in a little, while the

The simple passenger-side front door trim of a Jaguar 420, showing the window winder on the right, the door-opening handle on the left and the interior door lock above it, with the armrest and map pocket below.

Almost as soon as the S-type went into production, it received the revised horn button and steering column realignment in company with the Mark X and Mark 2 in October 1963. Radial-ply tyres were fitted as standard from the following month and both the S-type and Mark X had to have a recalibrated speedometer because of the tyres' reduced rolling radius. The automatic transmission was modified at the same time with a new relief valve to improve its change.

The Mark X's cooling system was revised in January 1964 with a new radiator and separate header tank, plus rerouted plumbing, to eliminate potential air locks. The grease nipples on the independent rear suspension's drive-shaft universal-joints were abandoned at the same time because frequently they had been neglected, leading to premature failure. Instead, the cars were fitted with sealed joints and dirt shields, which meant that they lasted longer without maintenance, but they still failed earlier

The dashboard of a Jaguar 420 showing its high-mounted electric clock in the centre of the padded surround and the neat location of the heater controls in the leading edge of the parcels tray.

other two remained in their original positions. The water jackets were changed for better circulation and a new crankshaft made to match the revised bores. New pistons were also fitted, but the same straight-port cylinder-head that had been used on the Mark X and the E-type was retained. The slightly realigned cylinders worked perfectly well with the original head. In this form, with triple SU carburettors, the 4.2-litre XK unit produced the same power as the 3.8-litre Mark X engine, 265 bhp, but the torque was better at 283 lb ft rather than 260 lb ft.

The 4.2-litre engine was fitted with a new water-heated inlet manifold and the Mark X received a revised cooling system with a viscous-coupling fan that saved 14 bhp at normal revs. A negative-earth electrical system was used with an alternator for better output and a pre-engaged Lucas starter motor was fitted to help cold-weather starting, the new gearbox housing being designed to accept this motor. On Mark Xs with automatic transmission the Model 8 Borg-Warner gearbox was fitted, which had 'Drive One' and 'Drive Two' positions on its control panel, enabling first gear to be used for maximum acceleration on take-off, or just the two top gears for the greatest smoothness. The new

The large, uncluttered luggage boot of a Jaguar 420, offering adequate space for large cases despite a stepped floor.

A concours-winning Jaguar 420 fitted with the smart optional chromed wire wheels and a Webasto sun roof.

transmission also incorporated an oil-cooler for safer towing.

The Varamatic power-assisted steering that was to be fitted to the Mark 2 from 1967 was used from the start of production on the 4.2-litre Mark X. The controversial Kelsey-Hayes servo was replaced with a more conventional line servo to give a better feel, and at the same time stronger calipers with a larger pad area were fitted. The road wheels had to be slightly reshaped to clear the new front-brake piping.

Considerable improvements were made to the standard of heating in the 4.2-litre Mark X by modifying the controls so that hot and cold air could be mixed, and by offering full air conditioning as an option. This Delaney Gallay system used an evaporator unit mounted in the boot and a refrigerator under the engine's radiator. In this way warm humid air was extracted from the interior of the car through vents in the rear parcel shelf and passed through the evaporator and refrigerator to be returned in a cooled and dehumidified state. The system was powered by an engine-driven compressor, which meant that a larger engine radiator and fan were needed.

Soon after the all-synchromesh gearbox had been offered as an option on the S-type, in December 1964, supplies built up sufficiently for it to be standardized on that model from March

The dashboard of the 420 G saloon showing its complicated heater controls on the lower parcel shelf rail. This car has been fitted with an optional steering lock and a tape player.

The Jaguar 420 G showing its revised radiator grille and indicator repeater light at the forward end of the chromed body line.

The eventual successor to the 420 and 420 G, the XJ6. This much-loved Series 1 saloon was a 4.2-litre automatic-transmission model driven by the author for more than 100,000 miles.

1965. Few changes took place to the S-type after that, the car having benefitted from the development work carried out on the Mark X and Mark 2. The only real changes were when the Mark 2's revised radiator and fan cowling were fitted in December 1965. Four months later the Mark X had its larger, air-conditioning type of radiator fitted as standard.

Major changes were afoot, however, with a revised model range being announced in October 1966. The S-type was modified to become either the Jaguar 420 or the Daimler Sovereign (depending on whose badges you fancied) and the Mark X became the 420 G (for Grand). The 420 G was hardly any different from the Mark X, having been redesignated primarily to help sales in the United States. It had a slightly facelifted exterior with a chrome strip and indicator-repeating lights along its sides, and a new radiator grille to match the 420. The wheel trims were modernized as well and some changes were made to the interior,

these being confined to the front seats, which were reshaped to give more lateral support, and to a padded top, which was fitted to the dashboard for safety, with a clock recessed in the centre. An electric rev counter replaced the cable-driven one in company with other Jaguars at that time.

The S-type featured many more changes, chiefly in styling and fitting the 4.2-litre engine in twin-carburettor form. The engine was the same as that fitted to the 4.2-litre Mark X (and the new 420 G) with a straight-port cylinder-head, but only two carburettors could be used because of the limited space available under the bonnet. In this form, its power output was rated at 245 bhp, rather than 265 bhp, with virtually the same torque. The styling changes, though confined to the front, were extensive. They followed closely on the Mark X and 420 G theme with a revised 'square' radiator grille and a four-headlamp system. The old Mark 2 and S-type bonnet was retained, however, rather than the full frontal-opening bonnet used on the Mark X and 420 G. This new frontal treatment made the underbonnet area longer, and allowed a new, larger, radiator to be fitted with room for optional air conditioning equipment similar to that offered on the Mark X.

The Varamatic power-assisted steering available on the Mark X could also be ordered now on the 420. The interior was revised along the lines of the 420 G but little else changed. The Daimler version of this Jaguar was almost identical except for a different radiator grille and badges. It cost more, however, and had power-assisted steering as standard and was not available in manual-gearbox form without overdrive.

These three cars continued in production substantially unaltered after their introduction. In company with other Jaguars, they received new inlet valve guide seals to reduce oil consumption in March 1967, a fuel filter from January 1968, and improved pistons in July 1968. The 420 G's engine mountings were revised to use the front subframe at the same time, which reduced even further any vibrations. The 420 was discontinued in September 1968 with the introduction of the superb new XJ6, while the Daimler Sovereign went on until August 1969, three months before the introduction of a Daimler version of the XJ6. Production of the 420 G carried on until June 1970, when the XJ6 lines got into full swing.

CHAPTER 5

The Daimler derivatives

1962 to 1969

The name of Daimler, which first appeared on a Jaguar-based saloon in 1962, is as old as the British motor industry itself. The company's first factory in a converted cotton mill in Coventry was established in 1896 to market, and soon to produce, British versions of the aristocratic German Daimler cars. The British firm's first consulting engineer was Frederick Simms, later to be acknowledged as the father of the British motor industry. They specialized in producing luxury cars and first-class commercial vehicles with aero engines at the factory in Allesley that later was to be acquired by Jaguar. Daimler had amalgamated with the Birmingham Small Arms Company after World War 1 and by 1960, Jaguar, still anxious to expand, bought the Daimler Company and Transport Vehicles (Daimler) from the BSA group. Two designs of car were part of the assets, the Daimler SP 250 sports car and the Majestic Majors in saloon and limousine forms. Both were powered by lightweight V-8 engines, a 2½-litre being used in the sports car and a 4½-litre in the large saloon and limousine.

The 2½-litre V-8 was especially interesting to Jaguar as it produced more power than their own 2.4-litre XK engine, weighed less and ran more smoothly. When it was tried in a hack Mark 1 saloon it transformed the car. Handling was much improved because the weight over the front wheels was reduced by 1.25 cwt to give approximately 52/48 per cent front/rear weight distribution against 55/45 for the 2.4-litre Mark 2 and 58/42 for the 3.4-litre model. The performance was also much improved because the engine was more powerful (producing 140 bhp against 120 bhp for the XK engine in 2.4-litre Mark 2 form) and gave more torque (155 lb ft against 140). The chief

disadvantage of this engine, and the 4½-litre V-8, was that it could be produced only in relatively small numbers unless a lot of capital was devoted to new tooling. The decision was taken, therefore, to install it in a Mark 2 bodyshell and sell the result as an upmarket derivative of the Jaguar 2.4-litre Mark 2. The Daimler name had long been associated with luxury cars of the highest quality and a gap had been left in the middle of the range by the demise of the early 2½-litre saloons in 1958. Ironically, it was the introduction of the Mark 1 Jaguar that had reduced demand for the similar-sized, but more expensive, Daimler Conquest Century, but there were still a lot of people who hankered after a medium-sized Daimler, so Jaguar decided to cash in on the demand.

The engine was built around a 90-degree cast-iron cylinder-block with aluminium heads and pushrods and valve rockers operated from a camshaft high in the centre of the vee. This engine, with a bore and stroke of 76.2 mm by 69.25 mm, had a capacity of 2,548 cc. It was designed by Edward Turner, who was responsible for the highly-successful 650 cc Triumph motorcycle vee-twin-cylinder engine. In many ways, the small Daimler V-8 resembled four Triumph motorcycle engines in line! Lightweight valve gear enabled as much as 7,000 rpm to be used with outstanding smoothness. The engine was modified slightly to fit in the Jaguar Mark 2 bodyshell, with a reshaped sump to clear the front suspension's cross-member and detail changes such as set bolts securing the cylinder-heads rather than studs, so that the heads could be removed while the engine was in the car. The only real compromise was seen in a very complicated twin exhaust system, the shape of which was dictated by the Mark 2 bodyshell's underside. Two SU carburettors were used.

A new and improved automatic transmission was fitted to the Daimler saloon, which was given the designation 2½-litre V-8. The automatic gearbox, a Borg-Warner Model 35, was shaped differently from the earlier Borg-Warner unit, which meant that a new, smaller transmission tunnel could be fitted, which allowed the Daimler's front seats to be extended inwards to form a split bench. As a result, three people could sit in the front at a squeeze. It was not thought at the time that potential Daimler owners would require the relatively unsophisticated manual transmission used on the Jaguar Mark 2 saloons. Legroom was of more importance, so the new seats were made thinner, with no picnic tables in the back, to leave more space for rear passengers, a modification that was to be carried over to the Jaguar S-type saloons the following year.

Softer front springs and dampers were used on the Daimler because of the reduction in weight over the front wheels. Many cars were supplied with power-assisted steering, although the manual-steering cars felt much better because of their weight distribution. They also used the optional Jaguar low rear axle ratio of 4.55:1 as standard because the engine could rev so freely, but although this gave excellent acceleration, fuel consumption suffered. Otherwise, the Daimler saloons were almost identical to the Jaguar Mark 2, apart from different badges and colour scheme options, plus a distinctive fluted-top version of the Jaguar Mark 2 radiator grille. The Daimler's performance was excellent, with a top speed of nearly 110 mph and a 0-60 mph time of 13.5 seconds — 14 mph faster than the 2.4-litre Mark 2 and 4 seconds quicker to 60 mph. Fuel consumption was not very impressive however, at 17 mpg overall, a figure which the 2.4-litre Mark 2 could beat by at least 2 mpg. The pricing of this new model was as competitive as ever, with a penalty of only about £100 over the 2.4-litre Mark 2 and a price about £20 less than that of a 3.4-litre Mark 2.

The early Daimler V-8 saloon, which was based so closely on the contemporary 2.4-litre Mark 2 Jaguar. The only real outward difference, apart from the badging, was the fluted radiator grille, following Daimler's traditional pattern, a fluted numberplate light and different twin-exhaust system.

Above, part of the special exhaust system on the 2½-litre V-8 saloon can be seen in this picture. Note the traditional Daimler 'D' on the wheel covers. Right, the compact V-8 engine linked to its normal automatic gearbox with the generator and induction system nestling in the top of the vee.

Few changes were made to the Daimler saloon other than to fit a higher rear axle ratio of 4.27:1 from January 1964. This increased the acceleration times by about 1 second up to 80 mph and made high-speed cruising much more relaxed, but more important, it reduced fuel consumption by about 2 mpg to roughly the same as that of the 2.4-litre Mark 2.

From October 1962, the Borg-Warner Model 35 automatic gearbox was fitted with 'Drive One' and 'Drive Two' ranges, in company with the Jaguar Mark X saloon. Most Daimlers continued to be made with leather upholstery, however, after the Mark 2 saloon was switched to Ambla in September 1966, because they normally appealed to a less cost-conscious sector of the motoring public. In September 1967, the Daimler 2½-litre V-8 underwent a similar facelift to the Jaguar Mark 2 saloons when they became the 240/340 range. This meant that the

The Daimler Sovereign, introduced in 1966, was virtually the same as the Jaguar 420 apart from its different grille and badges, but it was sold with a higher level of standard equipment.

would have meant expensive separate testing, precluded any such thoughts.

There was still a reasonably lucrative market for limousines in Britain, however, with Jaguar, Daimler and Austin — all of which became part of the British Leyland group in 1967 — competing with Rolls-Royce throughout the 1950s and 1960s. Daimler and Austin were the most successful at the bottom end of the market, with a few limousine versions of the Mark X and 420 G being sold alongside them. These Jaguars were normal Mark X or 420 G cars fitted with all the saloon models' optional extras and a special interior incorporating a division and bench seat for the driver and a front-seat passenger. The room in the front was rather restricted because pride of place was naturally given to the

Daimler — now called the V-8 250 — received the slim-line bumpers and revised valances front and rear, and a new set of hub caps. It kept its built-in foglamps, however, as a touch of luxury. Separate air filters were fitted to each carburettor in place of the old pancake one, which did a lot to improve accessibility under the bonnet. An alternator and negative-earth electrical system were also fitted, and the Varamatic power-assisted steering, which had been used on the Mark 2 saloons since July 1967, continued to be offered. A few V-8 250s were also fitted with the all-synchromesh Jaguar manual transmission with overdrive. The interior trim was also revised along the lines of the Jaguar 420 and Daimler Sovereign, which had been introduced the previous year. This meant that the V-8 250's dashboard had the padded top rail, a theme which was continued to the door trims, and a heated rear window was fitted as standard, along with reclining seats. In this form, the Daimler V-8 250 saloon continued in production until August 1969, when it had to make way for the new Daimler Sovereign. Very few V-8 250s were made in left-hand-drive form as the Daimler marque was not exported to the United States by Jaguar. At first this was because they were not made in sufficiently high quantities to justify marketing them in America, and then looming safety and environmental regulations, which

The interior of the Daimler limousine showing its comfortable main rear seat with one of the occasional seats erected. This is the standard model, which is used as a base for a wide variety of options that can be included in a custom-built interior.

The Jaguar XK-powered Daimler limousine, pictured in its 1980 form, was little changed after its introduction in 1968. The only really noticeable external alteration is the substitution of small rubber-faced buffers on the bumpers for the 420 G-style overriders used on earlier models.

A rear view of the 1980 Daimler limousine, showing to advantage its huge luggage boot and high roof line. The fluted numberplate light housing, which doubled as a handle for closing the boot lid, followed Daimler's traditional pattern. The car pictured is a standard model in black, although almost any colour scheme could be ordered. Some dual-tone examples have proved to be particularly attractive.

The XJ-style XK engine installation in the Daimler limousine. The engine is similar to that used in the Jaguar except that the Daimler name is moulded on one of the camshaft covers.

back-seat passengers, who had the benefit of such items as a cocktail cabinet built into the centre of the division. Sir William Lyons used one of these cars.

The Daimler Majestic Major, powered by the 4½-litre V-8 engine, was much more popular, as was the Austin Princess, of similar size. This was because they were far taller than the Mark X or 420 G, and offered easier entry and exit, as well as more legroom in the back. All three cars were discontinued in 1968, however, to be replaced by a special Daimler limousine based on 420 G components.

Pressed Steel Fisher, part of the British Leyland group, who made the 420 G bodyshell, sent the floor pressings, the front bulkhead and wheelarches to Motor Panels, of Coventry, who assembled them with an extra 1 ft 9 in of floor pan and sill-section behind the central door pillar. These sills were reduced in depth by 1.75 in in the area of the rear doors to make entry and exit easier than it had been in the 420 G, and the floor was reinforced in this area to make up for the resultant loss of rigidity. The front bulkhead was extended upwards and an entirely new body, as large as that of the old Austin Princess, which belittled even a Mark VII Jaguar, being built on the modified 420 G floorpan. Modern through-flow ventilation was incorporated at the same time, with an additional heater for the rear compartment fitted under the front seats. The engine, automatic transmission and suspension all came from the 420 G but, of course, a special propeller shaft was needed. Wherever possible, other items from the 420 G, such as the bumpers, were used to keep down costs. The twin petrol tanks were fitted in the rear wings to give an enormous luggage boot and Varamatic power-steering was supplied as standard. In company with the spring rates, the hydraulic assistance was increased to cope with the overall weight of 2 tons 3 cwt.

The new bodyshell was delivered unpainted to Vanden Plas coachworks, in London, also part of the British Leyland group, where the car was assembled, painted to the highest standards and trimmed. The new Daimler's interior followed the established lines of the Jaguar and the Austin Princess which had been made there previously. The radiator grille on the front was a larger addition of that fitted to the Daimler Sovereign. In this form, these cars were among the largest on the road in Britain, with an overall width of 6 ft 6.5 in, wheelbase of 11 ft 9 in, length of 18 ft 10 in and height of 5 ft 3.75 in. Only Rolls-Royces, costing nearly four times as much, could approach these eight-seaters in luxurious carrying capacity. Production of the Daimler limousine continued at Vanden Plas at the rate of about 10 per week until the works closed in 1979, when production was transferred to Coventry.

CHAPTER 6

Jaguar saloons in competition

Mark VII to Mark 2

Although Jaguar's reputation for producing cars of outstandingly high performance was established by their sports cars, such as the racing C-types and D-types and the road-going XKs, it was confirmed by their saloons powered by the same type of engine. The large saloons, such as the Marks VII, VIII and IX, were not rallied or raced extensively, but their achievements when they did appear were sufficiently dramatic that this did not matter; they contributed superbly to the Jaguar legend. The smaller saloons, the Marks 1 and 2, were far more suitable for circuit racing and they dominated touring car events from 1957 to 1962. No wonder they became so popular with bank robbers — they were demonstrably the fastest saloon cars on the road! They were a little too heavy for total success in international rallying during this period, however, although they had an outstanding run of victories in the touring car section of the Tour de France, which offered an important combination of rallying and circuit racing.

The Monte Carlo Rally was one of the most glamorous and important sporting events in the 1950s, at least the equal of Le Mans and the top Grands Prix in publicity value. This event is held, by tradition, in January, when the weather in the French Alps, which generally provides the most testing terrain of the course, is usually at its worst. The Mark VII Jaguar proved to be well suited to this event despite its great bulk. It was very heavy — around 34 cwt — but it had such good torque that it could simply plough its way through really deep drifts, and when it was on dry roads it was as fast, if not faster, than many of the GT cars. The first year in which Mark VIIs competed, 1952, was particularly bad so far as the snow was concerned, and trials expert Sydney Allard received tremendous publicity for winning

in a Ford V-8-engined car that he had built himself. Allard's firm was tiny, however, and could not produce many cars, so Jaguar felt more commercial benefit from the success achieved by their Mark VIIs in fourth (Cotton/Didier) and sixth places (Heurteux/Crespin).

Various other Mark VIIs finished well down, including one driven by Leeds Jaguar distributor Ian Appleyard, who shared his car with his wife, Pat, who was Sir William Lyons' daughter. The Appleyards, who were Britain's top rally team at the time, had achieved considerable success with an XK 120, but they stuck to their Mark VII for the Tulip Rally in the spring, and took second place behind Ken Wharton's Ford Consul.

At that time, production car racing was rapidly becoming popular in Britain, the premier event being held at Silverstone. At first, sports cars were allowed to enter and the Jaguar XKs made mincemeat of the opposition, but soon so many races were being organized for these cars that it was decided to confine the Silverstone event to saloon cars to make it different. The result was that a Mark VII in the hands of Stirling Moss won convincingly in 1952 and this time Allard was relegated to third place behind Wharton, who drove a Healey on this occasion.

The Appleyards came within one second of winning the Monte Carlo Rally in 1953 when good weather conditions allowed more than half the field to reach the final test unpenalized. The very experienced Dutchman, Maurice Gatsonides, won in a Ford Zephyr with Dubliner Cecil Vard fifth in an obsolete Mark V Jaguar. The Appleyards followed up this fine performance by taking fifth place in their Mark VII in the Tulip Rally, and by dint of excellent results in their XK 120 they finished second in

Tom McCahill, of the American magazine *Popular Mechanix*, prepares to set a record for stock saloon cars at Daytona Beach in 1951 with a Mark VII Jaguar, which recorded 100.9 mph despite poor conditions of soft sand and a high wind. McCahill is behind the wheel receiving instructions from the starter, Bob Stahl.

the European Touring Championship. Then Moss won the Silverstone production car race again in his Mark VII from Harold Grace's Riley RM. By 1953, Britain's economy was recovering from the ravages of war and the Silverstone event was assuming great importance to the public, with consequent benefit to Jaguar sales, particularly as a C-type had scored its second victory at Le Mans that year.

A Mark VII again came within seconds of winning the Monte Carlo Rally in 1954, when Ulsterman Ronnie Adams was only beaten in the last test of the Monaco Grand Prix circuit by local ace Louis Chiron in a Lancia Aurelia GT. Although he was handicapped down to sixth place because of engine capacity, Adams' handling of the bulky Mark VII was so spectacular that it gained excellent publicity for Jaguar. Vard was eighth in another Mark VII.

Three of these massive saloons, driven by Appleyard, Le Mans winner Tony Rolt and Moss, finished in line-ahead formation in the Silverstone production car race despite a stern challenge from a team of Daimler Conquests. Jaguar certainly treated this event seriously as they built a special magnesium-bodied Mark VII for

it, although it was not used when it became apparent that the existing steel-bodied Mark VIIs were still faster than the works Daimlers. Until then, Jaguar had been content to race their Mark VIIs with only minimal modifications, such as 210-bhp XK 120 engines and close-ratio gearboxes, stiffer shock absorbers and bucket seats, with little attention paid to weight-saving. But the Mark VII driven by Mike Hawthorn to victory in the 1955 Silverstone race used light-alloy panels, which had been made at the same time as the magnesium-bodied Mark VII had been constructed. This was a works car, registered LWK 343, which had already seen extensive use in the Monte Carlo Rally and at Silverstone. It was supported by similar Mark VIIs driven by Ian Stewart and Desmond Titterington in second and third places, with Wharton fourth in a Ford Zephyr. Mark VIIs also won the team award in the Monte Carlo Rally that year with Adams taking eighth place, Vard 27th and Mattock 37th.

By 1956, although Jaguar sports cars had won all manner of events, victory in the Monte Carlo Rally had eluded the Mark VII. However Adams changed all that with a glorious drive in company with Frank Biggar and Derek Johnston to win in a works car, registered PWK 700. It was the only machine of more than 2,500 cc to finish in the first 38 places — testimony to the marvellously consistent way in which it was driven in an event which handicapped large cars so heavily.

Soon after, Frank Grounds gave the Mark 1 saloon its first competition success, finishing fourth overall in the RAC Rally and winning the up-to-2,700 cc class. Two months later, in May, the Belgian driver Paul Frère gave the Mark 1 its first victory, in the Spa production car race. But Jaguar continued to race the Mark VII at Silverstone, two of the big saloons being provided for Frère and Ivor Bueb in the unlimited-capacity class and two 2.4-litre Mark 1s, for Mike Hawthorn and Duncan Hamilton, in the medium-sized class. It was just as well from the point of view of overall results because Hawthorn's Mark 1 dropped a valve and Hamilton's car was outpaced by the larger machines of Bueb, who scored a narrow victory over Wharton, who was driving a much-modified Austin A 90. Frère was fourth.

There was nothing that could stay with the Mark 1 in saloon car racing when the 3.4-litre model was introduced in 1957. Very early examples, such as that driven by Archie Scott-Brown in the Silverstone production car race, suffered from fading drum brakes, but disc-braked examples, such as those driven by Hawthorn, Bueb and Hamilton (who finished in that order in 1957) were immediate race-winners. In addition to their improved brakes, they had stiffened suspension, with heavier anti-roll bars, and a limited-slip differential. The engines and gearboxes were similar to those used in the racing Mark VIIs.

During the 1950s and 1960s, the Tour de France, featuring numerous circuit races and tortuous hill-climbs, coupled with closely-timed road sections, came to prominence in the rally world. At first it was weighted in favour of sports cars, but it was revised in 1957 to feature two categories, for GT and touring cars. There were to be two outright winners, and clearly Ferrari would dominate the GT classes. Obviously the 3.4-litre Mark 1 was a likely contender in the touring car classes, but Jaguar suffered bad luck when early leaders Hernano da Silva Ramos, Sir

Rally expert Ian Appleyard in his Jaguar Mark VII number 3, winning the Silverstone production car race in 1954 from Tony Rolt in the works car number 5, after Stirling Moss in another works Mark VII had had to free a jammed starter on the line. Moss went on to take third place.

Mike Hawthorn in his 3.4-litre Mark 1 saloon number 33 fights for the lead of the production car race at the International Trophy meeting at Silverstone in 1958 with Tommy Sopwith in his similar car number 34. Sopwith won on this occasion.

Only 22 of the 98 starters finished the 1958 Liège-Rome-Liège Rally — also called the Marathon de la Route — such was the toughness of the course and the high average speed demanded of the competitors. The German crew of Lindner and Walter, pictured here in their 3.4-litre Mark 1 saloon, tried gallantly, but failed to finish the event, which was won by Frenchmen Hebert and Consten in an Alfa Romeo Giulietta Sprint Zagato. Consten later switched to Jaguar saloons to become one of the most distinguished rally drivers, while Lindner became one of the most formidable circuit racers in Jaguar saloons and sports cars.

Above, Ronnie Adams swings to victory in the 1956 Monte Carlo Rally high in the hills above the Mediterranean resort. Right, the cockpit of his car, revealing relatively few modifications other than the addition of a second speedometer, a chronometer, a map tray and a light for the navigator and extra screen-demisting units.

Gawaine Baillie and Bernard Consten were all eliminated in 1957, and in 1958 similar troubles befell Tommy Sopwith and the Whitehead brothers, Peter and Graham, when leading, although Baillie took third place with Peter Jopp. It was not until 1959 that da Silva Ramos won at last to give Jaguar the first of a string of victories.

Meanwhile, Baillie's team leader, Tommy Sopwith, was dominating British saloon car racing with his 3.4-litre Mark 1, and won numerous events in both 1957 and 1958. Baillie was frequently second, but won once at Aintree when Sopwith's brakes failed, and the chief opposition to the Sopwith team came from another Jaguar entered by Guildford dealer John Coombs. This car was used by Jaguar works drivers Hamilton and Ron Flockhart, with Hamilton winning in one of his last races at Goodwood in 1958. 'It was amazing how you could throw these saloons about,' said Hamilton. Star drivers continued to make guest appearances in Coombs' cars, with Walt Hansgen — who normally drove Jaguars in America for Briggs Cunningham — winning at Silverstone after Sopwith lost a wheel. The loss of heavily-stressed wheels was not uncommon in touring car events

at the time before purpose-designed racing wheels were allowed. By the end of the season, Sopwith was level on points with Jack Sears, who drove the ex-Wharton Austin Westminster in the under-2,700 cc class, for the first British Saloon Car Championship. The result was that Sopwith and Sears had a run-off in BMC-loaned Riley 1.5s and Sears won, but Sopwith was content with his performances, although he announced his retirement from driving after winning at Snetterton the next week. He did not leave the sport, though, and continued as a leading Jaguar entrant with his Equipe Endeavour. He had also used his Mark 1 for the 1958 RAC Rally, in which he challenged Peter Harper's leading Sunbeam Rapier. It was in this event that the Suffolk farming twins, Don and Erle Morley, came to fame by winning their class in a 2.4-litre Mark 1.

The Monte Carlo Rally had been cancelled in 1957 because of the Suez fuel crisis, and snow and secret checks wrecked most of the Jaguar crews' chances in 1958. However, Bobby Parkes and George Howarth won their class in 1959 and took eighth place overall with Philip Walton and Michael Martin ninth in another 3.4-litre Mark 1. Eric Brinkman and John Cuff backed them up

Roy Salvadori, in John Coombs' 3.4-litre Mark 1 Jaguar, leads Sir Gawaine Baillie, in a similar car, at the Silverstone International Trophy meeting in 1959. Salvadori eventually finished second behind Ivor Bueb in another 3.4-litre Mark 1, with Baillie third.

A 3.4-litre Mark 1 Jaguar saloon did well in the 1959 Monte Carlo Rally with Bobby Parkes and George Howarth winning their class. However, Eric Haddon and Norman MacLeod, pictured here near Madamaire, were not so lucky and retired later in the event.

Twelve Jaguars were entered for the 1960 Tulip Rally — more than any other marque. Eric Haddon's XK 150S sports car was the best-placed, in 10th position, with Jim Boardman's 3.8-litre Mark 2 saloon 11th and Bobby Parkes, pictured here in a similar car, 17th.

in 37th place, which was sufficient to give Jaguar the prestigious Charles Faroux team award.

Then the Morley twins, who regarded the Tulip Rally as an annual pre-harvest holiday, took a brand-new 3.4-litre Mark 1 to a sensational overall win in 1959. Only five cars survived fearful weather conditions without penalty, and Donald Morley's brilliant driving won the rally on the last stage at the Zandvoort racing circuit. The 3.4-litre Mark 1's successes on the track continued unabated during 1959 with Bueb taking over as Sopwith team-leader and winning most races at speeds slightly higher than those achieved by his entrant the year before. He kept up Jaguar's string of wins in the Silverstone production car race from Roy Salvadori in Coombs' car, Baillie, Dick Protheroe and Tommy Dickson. Peter Blond was sixth overall and first in the under-2,700 cc class with his 2.4-litre car — one of the few times in which Jeff Uren's Ford Zephyr failed to win this smaller class. Such was the rivalry between the Jaguar drivers — particularly in the ultra-competitive Coombs and Sopwith cars — that none of them won sufficient points to take the British saloon car title, which went to the consistent Uren in his Zephyr.

The Mark 2 Jaguar made its competition debut in April 1960 in Australia in the hands of David MacKay, who had previously raced a 3.4-litre Mark 1. The chief opposition for this factory-prepared 3.4-litre Mark 2 in the Tasman series was provided by Ron Hodgson's 3.8-litre D-type-engined Mark 1. The 3.8-litre version of the Mark 2 made its British debut with Baillie at the wheel, finishing third behind Sears' Aston Martin DB4 and Protheroe's modified XK 120 at Aintree in May 1960.

As the top teams turned to Mark 2s, the old Mark 1s were taken over by drivers such as Bill Aston (in Baillie's car) and Peter Sargent (in the Coombs car). Although they looked almost the same as standard production cars, they were very different under the skin. The Coombs car, for instance, had a much-modified

Bernard Consten and Jack Renel head for victory in the 1961 Tour de France in one of their famous white 3.8-litre Mark 2 Jaguar saloons which swept all before them in the touring car class of this event between 1960 and 1963.

engine with 10:1 compression ratio, triple SU carburettors, oversize XK 120 sump, competition clutch, close-ratio gearbox, low rear axle ratio, limited-slip differential, lowered and stiffened suspension, wide rear track, strengthened bodyshell and alloy panels. The Mark 2s were modified in a similar way and they received a high-ratio Mark 1 steering box.

Salvadori won most races that year in the Coombs car, while a variety of drivers drove Sopwith's machine notably Stirling Moss and Jack Sears. Lotus constructor Colin Chapman made one guest appearance in the Coombs car and promptly won at Silverstone from Sears!

In rallying, the RAC event was switched to November and the regulations tightened to make it more attractive to star Continental drivers as a grand finale to the international season. More special stages were held off the road, to the detriment of Jaguar's chances, so the factory interest switched to the Tour de France. It was to be the start of four years of dominance in this event by the French team of Bernard Consten and Jack Renel. They were fanatics for preparation, spending days reconnoitring the course despite an encyclopaedic knowledge of the mountains in which the timed climbs were held, then driving with great consistency to take the lead in the touring car class as other less-disciplined drivers retired or made mistakes. Baillie and Jopp were second in class.

Jaguars were still suitable for the fast roads of the Alpine Rally, and in 1960 José Behra and René Richard won the touring car category and a Coupe des Alpes in a 3.8-litre Mark 2 in company with Bobby Parkes and Geoff Howarth in a similar car. They were third and fifth overall and won two of only six Coupes des Alpes to be awarded that year for unpenalized runs as, like the RAC Rally, this event had been tightened-up and made considerably tougher.

Circuit racing in 1961 was enlivened by a third team of 3.8-litre Mark 2s for Bruce McLaren, Dennis Taylor and occasionally John Surtees. They competed under the Peter Berry Racing banner and pressed the established teams close, although Roy Salvadori still won the majority of races for John Coombs, despite further strong opposition from Mike Parkes and Graham Hill, driving for Sopwith, while Chris Kerrison drove a 2.4-litre Mark 2 with some success in the smaller class. Jaguar were nearly beaten, however, in the Silverstone production car race by Dan

Jaguar had dominated the Silverstone production car race since its inception, but the marque nearly lost out in 1960 when Dan Gurney led in a massive Chevrolet Impala until one of its rear wheels collapsed. Gurney is seen here leading Mike Parkes' 3.8-litre Mark 2, with Roy Salvadori hanging on in a similar car after having had to stop to close his bootlid. Eventually, Graham Hill got past in his 3.8-litre Mark 2 to win from Parkes.

Jack Sears leads Equipe Endeavour teammate Mike Parkes during the Lombank Trophy meeting at Snetterton, in 1961, before both these Sopwith team cars ran out of petrol on the last lap, allowing former teammate Sir Gawaine Baillie to win in his private 3.8-litre Mark 2!

Gurney's huge Chevrolet Impala. This lumbering American giant, with half as much power again as the Jaguars, led them all until a wheel collapsed, after which Graham Hill won the event from Parkes with McLaren finishing third.

In Australia, Bob Jane raced a much-modified Mark 2 with an engine capacity increased to 4.2 litres. He won numerous races with this car, continuing to beat even the bigger V-8-engined cars as late as 1965. Jane visited Europe in 1962 and led at the British Grand Prix meeting, enraging most of the field by weaving from side to side down the straight to hinder overtaking; eventually he spun and retired with overheating. Jaguar saloons were winning everywhere in 1961 and 1962 with Larry Rodriguez Larretta and Jack Greene taking the Buenos Aires 500-miles production car race despite 25 wheel changes to replace worn-out tyres! Tyre consumption was a major problem for the Mark 2s in long-distance events, particularly the Tour de France.

Graham Hill joined Salvadori in Coombs cars in 1962, with Sears and Parkes continuing with Sopwith's Equipe Endeavour, and David Hobbs, Peter Woodroffe, Chris McLaren and Peter Dodd were amongst those who joined the ranks of Mark 2 drivers, although usually it was Hill or Salvadori doing the winning. Another warning of the transatlantic menace to come

Roy Salvadori, in Tommy Atkins' Mark 2 Jaguar, leads Mike Salmon's similar car through the Goodwood chicane in pursuit of eventual winner Graham Hill, in John Coombs' Mark 2, during the Easter 1963 meeting. This was the last good year for the Mark 2 in circuit racing.

Jaguar 3.8-litre Mark 2 saloons won the *Motor* Six-Hours touring car race at Brands Hatch in both 1962 and 1963, but the ex-Equipe Endeavour car of Chris Summers and Keith Wilson could manage only 17th place as the marque's sole survivor in 1964. The Mini-Cooper S, driven by John Handley and Ralph Broad, took seventh place and the Alfa Romeo Giulia TI Super, driven by Francesco de Leonibus and Riccardo di Bona, finished 15th. The winning car was a Lotus Cortina driven by Sir John Whitmore and Peter Procter.

was seen in the way in which Charles Kelsey in a Chevrolet Chevvy 2 beat Salvadori at Brands Hatch; it was to be the one and only time that the Chevvy beat the Jaguars in 1962, but it showed that it could be done.

In October, *The Motor* staged a six-hours race for Group 2 saloons — the modified class in which the Mark 2s raced — with a predictable Coombs-versus-Sopwith battle. Mike Salmon and Peter Sutcliffe led in their Coombs car for most of the race until Parkes and Jimmy Blumer got ahead of them by virtue of faster pit stops in the Sopwith car. Then Salmon retired with wheel bearing failure — showing how highly-stressed these cars were — and the Sopwith entry won easily from the German Mark 2 drivers, Peter Lindner and Peter Nocker.

Lindner, who had won his class at the Nurburgring in a 3.4-litre Mark 2 in 1961, continued with a works-prepared 3.8-litre in 1962 and 1963, dominating European saloon car racing. Their chief opposition came from Mercedes-Benz with their works-entered 300 SE saloons, although Nocker was consistently faster and went on to win the first European Touring Car Championship.

In the Tour de France there was trouble when Consten discovered that the works-prepared cars of Jack Sears and Claude Lego and Sir Gawaine Baillie and Peter Jopp had 2-inch SUs and the other Mark 2s had only 1.75-inch carburettors. The protest against the works cars was disallowed — the regulations were open to a variety of interpretations at that time — but Consten had consolation of winning in any case as crashes eliminated both Sears and Baillie.

Jaguar started the 1963 season successfully with Peter Sargent, John Bekaert, Geoff Duke, Peter Lumsden and Andrew Hedges breaking four International Class C records in a standard 3.8-litre Mark 2 by driving 10,000 miles at more than 106 mph throughout poor weather conditions at Monza. Sopwith had now withdrawn from the scene, Salvadori began to drive for magazine magnate Tommy Atkins, and with Hill in the Coombs Jaguar they continued their ding-dong battle until a 7-litre Ford Galaxie entered by Jeff Uren for the John Willment Organization intervened.

Baillie soon acquired another Galaxie and before long these enormously powerful cars were defeating the Mark 2s regularly,

Leicestershire Jaguar specialist Graig Hinton has become a prolific winner in classic saloon car events with his Mark VII saloon since this form of racing began in 1975. His well-prepared car, pictured here, presents a constant spectacle on the circuits, such is its bulk compared with most other racing saloons.

except in the rain, when the Jaguars left them floundering. One of the last great victories for the Mark 2 in circuit racing was by the Atkins car driven by Salvadori and Denny Hulme in the Brands Hatch six-hours race at the end of the season. They won from Lindner and Nocker after the former Coombs car driven by Salmon and Sutcliffe was disqualified for having an oversize inlet manifold. A new threat was heralded by Sears and Bo Ljungfeldt, who took third place in a Willment Ford Cortina GT.

Consten won the Tour de France for a fourth time, despite a determined bid by the Galaxies and Ford's new Lotus Cortina, and another distinguished French rally team, that of Annie Soisbault and Louisette Texier, was second in a 3.8-litre Mark 2. Consten stuck to Jaguar for 1964, but was relegated to third place by two of Ford's new compact Mustangs, although once again he showed himself to be king of the mountains. Texier and Marie-Louise Mermod won the ladies' award in the touring section with a 3.8-litre Mark 2. This was the last Tour de France for four years as the event had become too expensive to run. When Consten helped re-establish it in 1969 it became a Porsche benefit, showing how fast the competition motoring world changes.

Despite the V-8 and Lotus Cortina menace, which swept competitive Jaguars off the tracks in 1964, Nocker continued to race with some success in Europe and as late as 1966 the Franco/Belgian team of Robert Dutoit and Eddy Meert finished fifth overall in the Spa 24-hours race in a 3.8-litre Mark 2 that had been prepared as part of a rally team led by Consten in 1962. Jaguar saloon cars continued to race in club events until 1975, when once again they had a championship series to contest — for classic saloon cars. This 'poor man's formula' was confined to selected cars of a type built before 1957, thus excluding the rapid 3.4-litre Mark 1, but allowing in the popular 2.4-litre cars. The result was that Jaguars were to win most of these races for the next five years, usually with the Mark 1, but sometimes with a crowd-pleasing Mark VII driven by Graig Hinton. From domination to disappearance and back to domination, the classic Jaguar saloons have come full-circle in competition.

CHAPTER 7

The practical side

Maintenance and restoration

Practically every known problem with a classic saloon car can crop up with a Jaguar as many as 30 years old, but it can be useful to know what to look for in general, and to identify the most common problem areas, when buying such a machine or simply trying to keep it running. By the standards of the 1950s, the early Mark VII, VIII and IX saloons were exceptionally well-made. Their massive chassis are not particularly prone to rust and their bodies seem to survive especially well apart from the sills, wings and spare-wheel wells.

The mechanical side is equally strong, and the interior so well made that such cars in good, sound condition are not so rare as those of many other marques. The later Mark 1, Mark 2 and independent-rear-suspension saloons are just as good mechanically, but they tend to suffer more from terminal body rot because of their unitary construction. On the other hand, they are almost invariably younger than the Mark VII, VIII and IX saloons and, as a result, have suffered less from the ravages of time. Prices need not be high, either, by today's standards; Jaguars use a lot of petrol and can be expensive to run on an everyday basis, which helps to keep down their resale value.

The XK engines used in the classic Jaguar saloons are exceptionally durable units, which should be good for 100,000 miles without a major overhaul. But many of these cars will have covered more than that by now, so look out for general engine wear when inspecting a car. Clouds of blue smoke indicate bore or valve-guide wear, although a clean blue haze on acceleration is normal, especially with the 3.8-litre engine, which tends to burn more oil than the others.

The XK engines are often noisy at the top-end, but this need not be much of a problem. A considerable amount of noise can be caused by the top timing chain, which is easily adjusted to compensate for wear. Tappets take longer to adjust because of the twin overhead camshafts. The bottom timing chain and tensioner are much more of a problem, needing quite a lot of work to change. Generally, the Mark VII has a spring-bladed tensioner, which can break, and later cars have hydraulic tensioners which may be suffering only from a blockage in the timing chest oil feed, which is easily cleared. Camshaft wear is much more serious, as these are expensive items to replace. Camshaft covers frequently spring oil leaks, as well, because of incorrect tightening, particularly with those on the early Mark VIIs, which had fewer securing studs.

Bearing trouble is rare with an XK engine, such is the strength of the bottom-end, but listen for rumbling in any case, and watch the oil pressure like a hawk — it should be between 35 psi and 45 psi at 3,000 rpm when the engine is hot. Should the oil pressure gauge show unusually high or low readings, suspect trouble with the oil pressure relief valve, or with the sensor on late-model cars. A simple test with an independent gauge can confirm or deny engine or oil pressure gauge trouble. Alternatively, a worn oil pump can cause low oil pressure, which is far more easily cured than bearing trouble.

Overheating through old age or neglected maintenance is a common problem with Jaguars, so watch for tell-tale rust stains in the engine compartment, particularly around the core plugs. Misfiring is also a common problem, frequently caused by sparking plugs that have deteriorated; they can last as little as 6,000 miles on hard-driven cars. A lumpy tickover can be caused

The bare bodyshell of a Mark 1 saloon as it should appear. Sadly, corrosion strikes all round the outer limits of the body, except in the roof area.

by incorrect synchronization, or wear, in the carburettors. Jaguar exhausts tend to be extremely complicated and they tend not to last long if they are made of mild steel. Quite innocuous leaks can cause a dramatic loss of torque, so make sure that the exhaust is in good order before suspecting engine trouble. Stainless steel is not necessarily the answer to the exhaust problems on a Jaguar because some grades of this metal are prone to splitting with equally disastrous results for the engine's pulling power.

Similar comments apply to the V-8 engine in the Daimler 2½-litre saloon, except that it is far more prone to bearing trouble. The imminent demise of the bearings can be indicated by a drop in oil pressure on acceleration, even if the needle does return to normal almost immediately afterwards. Daimler engines have a tendency to smoke as well, with the valve guides being the most frequent culprits.

With a car so powerful and heavy as a Jaguar or Daimler saloon, clutch wear can present something of a problem on cars with a manual gearchange. Be prepared for this unit to need replacement in as little as 40,000 miles, although far higher mileages can be obtained with gentle and considerate use. As soon as any slip or

Once the metal has been cut back, the true extent of the problem is likely to become apparent. In this case the car was in a dangerous condition because the Panhard-rod attachment point could have broken as the car was driven at anything up to 125 mph.

The rear spring mounting box and Panhard-rod attachment point are particularly prone to corrosion, which may not appear to be too extensive until it is investigated thoroughly.

New metal sections can be fitted by specialists such as Classic Cars of Coventry, who supplied these pictures.

excess travel on the clutch pedal can be detected, the clutch plates must be replaced or the flywheel can be ruined. The engine and transmission need to be removed to change a clutch on most Jaguar saloons, so it is not a condition to be taken lightly.

The old-fashioned Moss gearbox without synchromesh on first gear is notorious for whining in first and reverse, but it is generally an extremely dependable unit. It loses a lot of the effectiveness in its synchromesh, particularly on second, at an early point in its life, so do not worry too much about replacement on that score. However, do worry about excessive noise, as spare parts are virtually unobtainable. The later all-synchromesh gearbox is entering this category now, but it should have good synchromesh on all gears. Be prepared for a slow, almost ponderous, gearchange on both boxes, however; this is quite normal, and rushing a gearchange is little advantage because there should always be lots of torque available with an XK engine.

Watch carefully for transmission slip with the Borg-Warner Model DG automatic gearbox — this was the unit used on Jaguar saloons before the adoption of the 'Drive One-Drive Two' range. These gearboxes can be prone to leakage and parts are scarce. By contrast, the rear axles are exceptionally reliable and long-surviving, hardly ever giving problems, even in extreme old age. The only common problem with the final-drive is experienced on the independent-rear-suspension saloons, where heat from the inboard brakes and final-drive can lead to premature deterioration of the differential oil seals, resulting in leakage.

The entire rear suspension has to be removed to attend to these seals, but it need not be a condition that must have urgent attention if the oil level of the final-drive is kept topped-up and the leaking oil does not find its way on to the brake discs. The universal-joints in these systems also have only a limited life and it is essential that they are kept in good condition for the security of the rear suspension.

It is also essential that the rubber suspension mountings are kept in good condition on all Jaguar and Daimler saloons for the sake of safety and good handling and ride. They must be replaced at the first sign of splitting or general deterioration. Shock absorbers generally last about 40,000 miles, or so, and have a substantial influence on the handling, comfort and ride, which might not be realized at first. Springs usually last a good deal

Once the new suspension mounting points have been fitted, more new metal is welded in to repair the inner wing.

Areas which tend to split, such as the vertical joint shown here, can be plated. These corrosion areas are common to both the Mark 1 and Mark 2 saloons. These illustrations are of a Mark 1.

longer, although there is a tendency for the top leaves to break on the Jaguar Mark 1, 2, 240 and 340 saloons and on the Daimler 2½-litre V-8. This condition is easily detected by a lopsided look to the way the car stands. The front coil springs on cars fitted with this suspension medium, particularly the 420 and Daimler Sovereign with the heavy 4.2-litre engine in a relatively light shell, deteriorate quicker than the four-coil system at the back, making the car look low at the front. In extreme cases, the front wheels can hit the wing wheelarches on full lock. Replacement of the springs, and almost inevitably the shock absorbers, is the only cure in such cases. The torsion bars at the front of cars fitted with this suspension medium hardly ever give trouble and in any case are adjustable. Wear in the ball-joints of old Jaguars is common because of poor maintenance. The steering gear fitted to unassisted cars is quite reliable, although the power steering has a tendency to develop leaks, as does its pump; listen for hissing noises here, watch for leaks, and feel for heaviness or non-

Only when a corroded saloon's body is stripped down is the extent of trouble at the front most readily apparent.

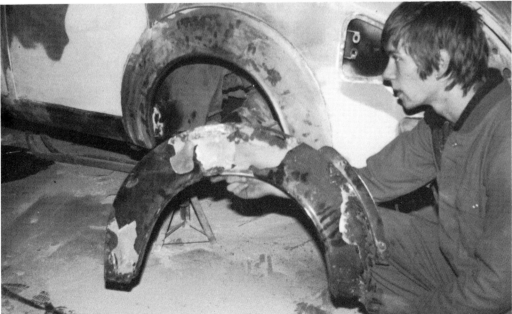

The wheel spats on the Mark 1 and Mark 2 saloons are a common corrosion point, rarely lasting as long as any other part of the bodyshell. The only real cure for extensive corrosion like this is replacement.

effectiveness of the assistance to the steering. Such conditions are expensive to cure.

The drum brakes fitted to the early saloons give few problems other than those associated with general wear. The disc-braked cars sometimes seize wheel cylinders, particularly when used on salty roads without being cleaned frequently afterwards. The oil seals on the rear cylinders of the independent-rear-suspension saloons frequently fail at around 80,000 miles, with a gradual loss of braking as the fluid swamps the discs. The rear suspension has to be removed to attend to such cases, and any braking defects can be expensive to repair. Rusty discs, caused by the seizure of a wheel cylinder, sometimes crack, so it is worth attending to these matters immediately. Frequently, the first effects of wheel-cylinder seizure are felt in uneven braking, which can also be caused by uneven pad wear. The brakes on a Jaguar saloon should never feel heavy. If they do, this condition is frequently caused by corrosion of the brake servo, particularly in the Mark 1s fitted with disc brakes, and the Mark 2s and their derivatives. This is

New sections can be fitted to old wings once the underlying trouble has been corrected. It is then essential to have the car comprehensively rust-proofed to prevent a recurrence of such corrosion and to have the rust-proofing process repeated at intervals, as recommended by specialists.

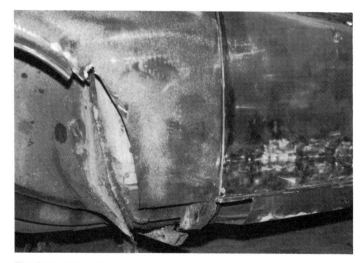

The front wing edges and inner splash panels have been cut away on this Mark 1 saloon in preparation for replacement of the corroded metal. It is essential during this operation that the entire body finish is removed to check for further corrosion. Removing all the paint, undercoat and so on is a lengthy and laborious process.

because their servo is mounted in an exposed position in one front wing in front of the road wheel. Generally sluggish reactions in the hydraulic systems for the brakes or clutch can be caused by old fluid absorbing water. If the fluid is in this state it must be changed, and so should the seals in any system that has been badly affected in this way.

The sidelamp nacelles and the front wing ventilator boxes are notoriously prone to suffer from corrosion, and the sliding roof's channels must be kept clean. The heavy doors have a tendency to sag on their overloaded hinges, and all forms of rubber insulation around the doors deteriorates. Anything to do with body repairs can be very expensive, even the rubber sealing if it needs replacement. The same goes for the interior, which can cost a fortune to restore, with bills running to four figures, such is the expanse — and expense — of leather. Deterioration of the woodwork is quite common in old age as well, but generally these veneers are easily detachable and can often be successfully renovated by french polishing. The electrical systems present few problems for specialists to repair, although they can be extremely

A typical example of corrosion in the front wings of a Jaguar saloon. Normally this area would have been covered by the outer wing.

Major surgery frequently reveals that the entire front crossmember and bumper support is about to disappear.

The car takes shape again during final assembly with a new crossmember and bumper support.

The massively constructed Mark X and 420 G bodyshell suffers less than the smaller classic Jaguar saloons from corrosion. Often, such trouble areas are confined to the sills, shown here, and the outer wings and luggage boot.

A new zinc-coated inner still section has been fitted to this Mark X bodyshell. The outer sill is welded on top.

unreliable on occasions if any components are in poor condition.

Many of these comments and warnings apply to the smaller unitary-construction saloons, of course, but they also have some special problems of their own. The condition of the sills is far more important on these models because they are such an essential part of the load-bearing structure. The problem here is that when the cars were built there was little effective rust-proofing and corrosion attacked the box-section members from the inside. What little paint was attached to the inside surfaces of the metal was burnt-off at the places where the metal was bent — and at its thinnest — by the welding used in the cars' construction. The only permanent cure after extensive and expensive replacement, should that be necessary, is frequent treatment with modern rustproofing materials.

Sometimes, the first evidence of extensive corrosion in the sills can be the collapse of the car's jacking points. The wings and valances are also notoriously prone to rust; the front valance behind the bumper is an area particularly badly affected. It is in this area that the servo's vacuum tank can rot through or fall off, and the chassis cross-member in front of the engine can also be badly affected by clumsy jacking or accident damage because of its exposed position. The front wings rot everywhere, particularly around the sidelamp nacelles and other light housings. The lips around the wheelarches also hold mud and road debris, which

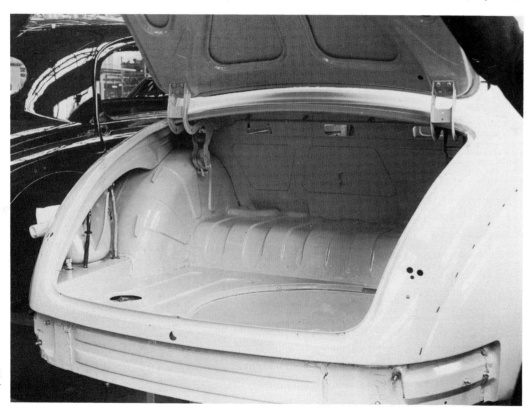

The Mark 1 bare bodyshell as it should look. This is also a common area for corrosion.

Typical corrosion areas in the Mark X bodyshell are highlighted by where the paint has been removed on this example.

leads to corrosion, and so does the rear plate behind the front wheels, which is insulated from the front wings by a rubber sealing strip. Often, this rubber strip deteriorates or is displaced, with the result that moisture and debris penetrates the rear of the wing, with resultant rot which also attacks the front of the sills.

The rear of the car suffers in similar vein, even on the independent-rear-suspension saloons with their reinforcements to the bodyshell. The rear valances and wing lips, and especially the spats where fitted, suffer badly from corrosion, as do the door shut faces. The far corners of the boot floor where the shock absorbers are mounted can be a special danger area. The spare-wheel well and wheelarch seams are other vulnerable points, as are the fuel tanks. The rear spring hanger boxes and Panhard rod mountings must also be in good condition for safety. Rot in the rear seat pan falls into the same category. The bottom half of the doors can suffer badly from corrosion, although this is less serious and not too difficult to repair.

It must be remembered that virtually any work to a classic Jaguar saloon can turn out to be much more expensive than might be thought at first because of the nature of the corrosion involved; corrosion in such a saloon can be like an iceberg with only a small percentage of its true area showing. As a result it is well worth sticking out for a car that has been kept in first-class condition rather than one which 'just needs a little bit of work on the body'.

CHAPTER 8

Sport and fellowship

The Jaguar clubs

The Jaguar Drivers' Club, which caters for the cars covered in this book, is one of the largest in the world with more than 6,000 members. It organizes social functions, race meetings, sprints, hill-climbs, national and international jamborees and spares-exchange days and produces an excellent monthly magazine, called the *Jaguar Driver*. In addition, the full-time staff at the Jaguar Drivers' Club headquarters help with information for members on all kinds of problems associated with buying, selling and running a Jaguar. The more specialized individual needs of the members are catered for by Registers — which amount to clubs within the parent club — of which the Mark VII, VIII and IX Register, the Mark 1 and 2 Register, and the S-type Register (which deals also with all independent-rear-suspension Jaguar saloons) will be of special interest to the readers of this book. The other registers, incidentally, are the SS Register for the early cars, the XK Register for XK sports cars, the E-type Register for the later sports cars and the XJ Register for the owners of recent Jaguar saloons.

The Jaguar Drivers' Club as it exists today was formed by a nucleus of XK owners in 1955. It developed from there to embrace all kinds of Jaguar and SS cars, organizing regular monthly meetings in 30 areas throughout Britain. These centres organized such events as barbeques, driving tests, quizzes and dinners for members, who own a wide variety of Jaguars. The Registers organize events — particularly jamborees — for the owners of their specific type of car, which owners of other Jaguar and SS cars can attend as guests. In addition, the Jaguar Drivers' Club organizes national functions, such as film shows and dinners, for all members and supplies a club caravan to tour events with merchandise associated with the cars to supplement the wares on display at trade stands. The club also helps members arrange specialized insurance at the most advantageous rates.

There are a large number of Jaguar clubs overseas, particularly in the United States and Australia, where so many cars were exported and where, because of the generally favourable climate, they have survived in large numbers. These clubs are organized mostly on an individual basis because of the substantial distances between their centres of membership. They are nearly all affiliated to a national organization, however, such as the Jaguar Clubs of North America, and have at least one national day for which members often travel vast distances to attend and exchange information and spares with other members.

The JCNA publishes a quarterly magazine called *Jaguar Journal*, which does a great deal to help keep membership together when the physical difficulties of great distances intrude. There is also a well-developed commercial club in the United States called the Eastern Jaguar Automobile Group of North America, whose membership extends to Europe, Australia, Asia and Africa. EJAG, as it is called, publishes a popular monthly magazine called *EJAG News*. This publication, like the *Jaguar Driver* and *Jaguar Journal*, carries articles on maintenance and restoration, descriptions of Jaguar events, product and book reviews, stories by Jaguar personalities, parts and service recommendations and advertising. Individual registers, centres and so on also produce their own newsheets, using similar information.

There are many specialists ready to supply spares for Jaguars or to do work on them, whose addresses would be too numerous to

On this and the next six pages are pictures of a typical selection of painstakingly prepared cars which appeared at a Jaguar Drivers' Club meeting. This example is a Jaguar Mark VIIM.

list here, but can be obtained from the Jaguar Drivers' Club headquarters at Jaguar House, 18 Stuart Street, Luton, Bedfordshire, England (telephone: Luton 419332). The addresses of other associations are:

The Jaguar Clubs of North America, Fred Horner, General Delivery, Holmes Beach, Florida 33509, USA; EJAG North America, Box J, Carlisle, Massachusetts 01741, USA.

The Jaguar Drivers' Club of Australia (New South Wales), PO Box 2, Drummoyne, NSW 2047, Australia; the Jaguar Drivers' Club of Western Australia, 20 Short Street, Joondanna 6060, Western Australia; the Jaguar Drivers' Club of Southern Australia, PO Box 30, Rundel Street, Adelaide, Southern Australia 5001; the Jaguar Car Club of Victoria, Box 161, Ringwood, Victoria 3134; the Jaguar Car Club of Tasmania, PO Box 131, North Hobart, Tasmania 7000; Jaguar Drivers' Club of Canberra, Box 400, Kingston, ACT 2604; the Classic Jaguar Club of Western Australia, 3 Bowden Street, Langford, Western Australia 6155.

Jaguar Drivers' Club Belgium, 30 Chemin des Deux Maisons-Box 9, 1200 Brussels. Jaguar Drivers' Club France, 39 Avenue de Laumiere, Paris 19. Jaguar Drivers' Club Germany, 18 Beethoven Street, 8011 Vatertetten, West Germany. Jaguar Drivers' Club Holland, Dr J. A. van Duren, Voorzitter, Witteven 8, 7963 RB, Ruimen, Holland. Jaguar Drivers' Club Italy, Roberto Causo, Via Condotti 91, Roma 00187. Jaguar Drivers' Club Norway, Postboks 1748 VIKA, Oslo 1. Jaguar Drivers' Club Sweden, Svenska Jaguar Klubben, Box 42092, 126 12 Stockholm 42. Jaguar Drivers' Club Denmark, Jens Roder, Lindevej 3A, 3060 Espergaerde, Denmark. Jaguar Drivers' Club Switzerland, Aldo Vinzio, BP 34-1211, Geneva 17.

Jaguar Drivers' Club South Africa, 30 Ballyclare Drive, Bryanston, Sandton, South Africa.

Jaguar Drivers' Club Brazil, William G. Halberstadt, Rua Haddock Lobo 281, Sao Paulo, SP 01414, Brazil.

Jaguar Drivers' Club Canada, Ian Newby, 6362 Chatham Street, West Vancouver, British Columbia.

Jaguar Drivers' Club New Zealand, PO Box 23-139, Papatoetoe, Auckland.

A Jaguar Mark IX.

A Jaguar Mark 1.

A Jaguar Mark 2.

A Jaguar S-type.

A Jaguar 240.

A Jaguar 420.

A Jaguar 420 G.

Technical specifications

Mark VII

Engine: 6-cyl, 83 × 106mm, 3,442cc, compression ratio 8:1 (7:1 optional), 2 SU carbs, 160bhp at 5,200rpm (150bhp with 7:1 CR), maximum torque 195lb ft at 2,500rpm.
Transmission: Axle ratio 4.27:1. Overall gear ratios: (manual, without overdrive) 4.27, 5.84, 8.48, 14.4; (overdrive) 3.54, 4.55, 5.5, 7.96, 13.6; (automatic) 4.27, 13.1-6.12, 21.2-9.86.
Suspension and brakes: Ifs, torsion bars, wishbones; live rear axle, half-elliptic leaf springs. Recirculating-ball worm-and-nut steering. Hydraulic drum brakes all round. 6.70-16in tyres on 5K rims (5.5K from late-1952), pressed-steel wheels.
Dimensions: Wheelbase 10ft; front track 4ft 8in (4ft 8.5in from June 1952); rear track 4ft 9.5in (4ft 10in from June 1952); length 16ft 4.5in; width 6ft 1in; height 5ft 3in; unladen weight 34.5cwt. Basic price on introduction £1,276.

Mark 1 2.4-litre

Engine: 6-cyl, 83 × 76.5mm, 2,483cc, compression ratio 8:1 (7:1 optional), 2 Solex carbs, SU optional, 112bhp at 5,750rpm, maximum torque 140lb ft at 2,000rpm.
Transmission: Axle ratio 4.55:1 (4.27 from June 1956). Overall ratios: (4.55 axle) 4.55, 6.22, 9.01, 15.35; (4.55 overdrive) 3.54, 4.27, 5.84, 8.46, 14.4; (automatic) 4.27, 13.2-6.14, 21.2-9.86.
Suspension and brakes: Ifs, coil springs, wishbones; live rear axle, radius arms, Panhard rod, half-elliptic leaf springs. Recirculating-ball worm-and-nut steering. Hydraulic drum brakes all round, discs all round optional from late-1957. 6.40-15in tyres on 5K rims, pressed-steel wheels (5K-15 wire wheels optional).
Dimensions: Wheelbase 8ft 11.375in; front track 4ft 6.625in; rear track 4ft 2.125in; length 15ft 0.75in; width 5ft 6.75in; height 4ft 9.5in; unladen weight 27cwt. Basic price on introduction £1,344.

Mark VIIM

Engine: As Mark VII except 190bhp at 5,500rpm, maximum torque 203lb ft at 3,000rpm.
Transmission: As Mark VII except (manual, without overdrive) overall ratios: 4.27, 5.17, 7.47, 12.73; (overdrive) 3.54, 4.55, 5.5, 7.96, 13.56, optional 3.54, 4.55, 6.22, 9.017, 15.35.
Suspension, brakes and dimensions: As Mark VII except, unladen weight 34.75cwt. Basic price on introduction £1,616.

Mark VIII

Engine: As Mark VII except 210bhp at 5,500rpm, maximum torque 216lb ft at 3,000rpm.
Transmission, suspension, brakes and dimensions as Mark VII except unladen weight 36cwt. Basic price on introduction £1,830.

Mark 1 3.4-litre
Engine: As Mark VIII.

Transmission: Axle ratio (manual, without overdrive, and automatic): 3.54; (overdrive) 3.77. Overall gearing: (3.54) 3.54, 4.541, 6,584, 11.95 (3.54 optional close-ratio gearbox) 3.54, 4.28, 6.2, 10.55; (3.77) 2.933, 3.77, 4.836, 7.012, 12.73; (3.77 optional close-ratio gearbox) 2.933, 3.77, 4.561, 6.597, 11.23; (automatic) 3.54, 10.95-5.08, 17.6-8.16.

Suspension, brakes and dimensions: As 2.4-litre Mark 1 except unladen weight 28.5cwt. Basic price on introduction £1,672.

Mark IX
Engine: 6-cyl, 87 × 106mm, 3,781cc, compression ratio 8:1 (7:1 optional), 2 SU carbs, 220bhp at 5,500rpm, maximum torque 240lb ft at 3,000rpm.

Transmission: As Mark VIII except overall gearing (automatic) 4.27, 13.2-6.14, 21.2-9.86.

Suspension: As Mark VIII.

Brakes: Discs all round.

Dimensions: As Mark VIII except unladen weight 35.5cwt. Basic price on introduction £1,994.

Mark 2 2.4-litre
Engine: 6-cyl, 83 × 76.5mm, 2,483cc, compression ratio 8:1 (7:1 optional), 2 Solex carbs, 120bhp at 5,750rpm, maximum torque 144lb ft at 2,000rpm.

Transmission: Until September 1965, axle ratio (manual, without overdrive, and automatic) 4.27; (overdrive) 4.55. Overall ratios: (manual, without overdrive) 4.27, 5.48, 7.94, 14.42; (overdrive) 3.54, 4.55, 5.84, 8.46, 15.36; (automatic) 4.27, 13.2-6.14, 21.2-9.86; from September 1965, axle ratio (overdrive) 3.54. Overall ratios: 3.54, 4.55, 5.78, 7.92, 12.19.

Suspension and brakes: As Mark 1, discs all round.

Dimensions: Wheelbase 8ft 11.375in; front track 4ft 7in; rear track 4ft 5.375in; length 15ft 0.75in; width 5ft 6.75in; height 4ft 9.75in; unladen weight 28.5cwt. Basic price on introduction £1,534.

Mark 2 3.4-litre
Engine and transmission: As 3.4-litre Mark 1.

Suspension, brakes and dimensions: As 2.4-litre Mark 2 except for unladen weight 29.5cwt. Basic price on introduction £1,669.

Mark 2 3.8-litre
Engine: As Mark IX.

Transmission, suspension, brakes and dimensions: As 3.4-litre Mark 2 except for unladen weight 30cwt. Basic price on introduction, £1,779.

Mark X 3.8-litre
Engine: As Mark IX except 3 SU carbs, 265bhp at 5,500rpm, maximum torque 260lb ft at 4,000rpm.

Transmission: As Mark VIII standard ratios.

Suspension and brakes: Ifs, wishbones, coil springs; irs, wishbones, radius arms, coil springs. Discs all round.

Dimensions: Wheelbase 10ft; front track 4ft 10in; rear track 4ft 10in; length 16ft 10in; width 6ft 4in; height 4ft 6.75in; unladen weight 37cwt. 7.50-14in tyres on 5.5K pressed-steel wheels. Basic price on introduction £2,392.

Daimler 2½-litre V-8
Engine: V-8cyl, 76.2 × 69.85mm, 2,548cc, 140bhp at 5,800rpm, maximum torque 155lb ft at 3,600rpm.

Transmission, suspension, brakes and dimensions: As 2.4-litre Mark 2 except unladen weight 28cwt. Basic price on introduction £1,239.

S-type 3.4-litre
Engine and transmission: As 3.4-litre Mark 2.

Suspension and brakes: As Mark X.

Dimensions: Wheelbase 8ft 11.5in; front track 4ft 7.25in; rear track 4ft 6.25in; length 15ft 7in; width 5ft 6.25in; height 4ft 7.75in; unladen weight 32cwt. 6.40-15in tyres on 5K pressed-steel wheels (5½K wire wheels optional). Basic price on introduction £1,669.

S-type 3.8-litre
Engine and transmission: As 3.8-litre Mark 2.
Suspension, brakes and dimensions: As 3.4-litre S-type except unladen weight 33cwt. Basic price on introduction £1,758.

Mark X 4.2-litre
Engine: 6-cyl, 92.07 × 106mm, 4,235cc, compression ratio 8:1 (7:1, 9:1 optional), 3 SU carbs, 265bhp at 5,400rpm, maximum torque 283lb ft at 4,000rpm.
Transmission: Axle ratio 3.54 (manual, without overdrive, and automatic), 3.77 (overdrive). Overall ratios (manual) 3.54, 4.7, 6.98, 10.76; (overdrive) 2.93, 3.77, 5.0, 7.44, 11.46; (automatic) 7.08-3.54, 10.33-5.16, 17.0-8.5.
Suspension, brakes and dimensions: As 3.8-litre Mark X. Basic price on introduction £2,156.

420G
As 4.2-litre Mark X except price on introduction £2,237.

420
Engine and transmission: As 4.2-litre Mark X except 2 SU carbs, 245bhp at 5,500rpm, maximum torque 283lb ft at 3,750rpm.
Suspension, brakes and dimensions: As 3.8-litre S-type saloon except basic price on introduction £1,930.

Daimler Sovereign
As 420 except basic price on introduction £2,064.

240
Engine: As 2.4-litre Mark 2 except 2 SU carbs, 133bhp at 5,500rpm, maximum torque 146lb ft at 3,700rpm.
Transmission: As post-September 1965 2.4-litre Mark 2.
Suspension, brakes and dimensions: As 2.4-litre Mark 2 except length 14ft 11in, basic price on introduction £1,365.

340
Engine and transmission: As 3.4-litre Mark 2.
Suspension, brakes and dimensions: As 240 except unladen weight 30cwt, basic price on introduction £1,442.

Daimler limousine
Engine and transmission: As 420 automatic.
Suspension and brakes: As 420G.
Dimensions: Wheelbase 11ft 9in; front track 4ft 10in; rear track 4ft 10in; length 18ft 10in; width 6ft 5.5in; height 5ft 3.75in; unladen weight 42.75cwt, basic price on introduction £3,824.

APPENDIX B

Chassis Number sequences — by model and date

Model	Years built	Numbers made	Chassis numbers from	Model	Years built	Numbers made	Chassis numbers from
Mark VII	Oct 50-Sept 54	12755 8184	710001 RHD 730001 LHD	Daimler 2 ½ -litre V-8	Nov 62-Aug 67	3376 621	IA 10001 RHD IA 20001 LHD
Mark VIIM	Oct 54-Jul 56	7245 2016	722755 RHD 738184 LHD	3.4-litre S-type	Sept 63-Aug 68	8665 1371	IB 1001 RHD IB 25001 LHD
2.4-litre Mark 1	Sept 55-Sept 59	16250 3742	900001 RHD 940001 LHD	3.8-litre S-type	Sept 63-Jun 68	9717 5418	IB 50001 RHD IB 75001 LHD
Mark VIII	Oct 56-Dec 59	4644 1688	760001 RHD 780001 LHD	4.2-litre Mark X	Oct 64-Sept 66	3720 1960	ID 50001 RHD ID 75001 LHD
3.4-litre Mark 1	Mar 57-Sept 59	8945 8460	970001 RHD 985001 LHD	Daimler Sovereign	Aug 66-Jul 69	5475 354	IA 3001 RHD IA 70001 LHD
Mark IX	Oct 58-Sept 61	5984 4021	770001 RHD 790001 LHD	420G	Oct 66-Jun 70	5429 1125	GID 53720 RHD GID 76961 LHD
2.4-litre Mark 2	Oct 59-Sept 67	21768 3405	100001 RHD 125001 LHD	420	Oct 66-Sept 68	7172 2629	IF 1001 RHD IF 25001 LHD
3.4-litre Mark 2	Oct 59-Sept 67	22095 6571	150001 RHD 175001 LHD	Daimler V-8 250	Jul 67-Aug 69	4779 104	IK 1001 RHD IK 0001 LHD
3.8-litre Mark 2	Oct 59-Sept 67	15383 14758	200001 RHD 210001 LHD	240	Sept 67-Apr 69	3716 730	IJ 1001 RHD IJ 30001 LHD
3.8-litre Mark X	Oct 61-Aug 64	9129 3848	300001 RHD 350001 LHD	340	Sept 67-Sept 68	2265 535	IJ 50001 RHD IJ 80001 LHD

How fast? How economical? Performance figures

	Mark VII (manual)	Mark VII (overdrive)	Mark VIIM (overdrive)	Mark VII (automatic)	Mark VIII (automatic)	Mark IX (automatic)	3.8 Mark X (overdrive)
Test source	*Autocar* 1952	*Autocar* 1954	*Motor* 1955	*Autocar* 1956	*Autocar* 1958	*Autocar* 1959	*Motor* 1964
Mean max speed (mph)	103	102.1	104.3	100.1	106.5	114.4	120
Accleration (sec)							
0-30	4.2	4.4	4.5	4.8	4.4	4.2	3.6
0-40	—	—	6.9	—	—	5.9	6.1
0-50	9.3	9.9	9.8	10.1	8.7	8.5	8.4
0-60	13.4	13.6	14.1	14.3	11.6	11.3	10.8
0-70	17.7	18.5	19.0	19.3	15.2	14.8	15.0
0-80	23.9	25.7	26.5	26.8	20.2	18.6	19.4
0-90	32.7	35.8	33.4	38.6	26.7	25.9	24.8
0-100	—	—	—	—	35.7	34.8	32.9
0-110	—	—	—	—	—	—	—
Standing ¼-mile (sec)	19.3	19.3	19.5	19.7	18.4	18.1	18.4
Overall fuel consumption (mpg)	19	20	18.8	18.5	17.9	13.5	13.6

	3.8 Mark X (automatic)	4.2 Mark X (overdrive)	4.2 Mark X (automatic)	2.4 Mark 1 (manual)	2.4 Mark 1 (overdrive)	3.4 Mark 1 (overdrive)	3.4 Mark 1 (automatic)
Test source	*Autocar* 1963	*Autocar* 1966	*Autocar* 1965	*Road & Track* 1956	*Motor* 1956	*Autocar* 1958	*Motor* 1957
Mean max speed (mph)	119.5	122.5	121.5	101.1	101.5	120	119.8
Acceleration (sec)							
0-30	4.9	3.9	4.0	4.3	4.6	3.1	4.5
0-40	6.7	5.8	5.6	7.0	6.9	—	6.5
0-50	9.1	7.9	7.2	10.0	11.0	7.0	8.7
0-60	12.1	10.4	9.9	13.1	14.4	9.1	11.2
0-70	15.1	13.6	12.8	17.5	19.9	12.4	14.2
0-80	20.6	17.1	17.0	24.2	28.6	16.0	17.9
0-90	26.3	22.5	21.9	35.0	39.1	20.5	23.0
0-100	33.3	29.5	27.4	—	—	26.0	30.3
0-110	44.9	40.3	36.5	—	—	34.6	—
Standing ¼-mile (sec)	18.5	17.4	17.0	19.0	19.6	17.2	18.0
Overall fuel consumption (mpg)	14.1	16	14.5	19.5 (US)	18.25	16	19.25

	2.4 Mark 2 (overdrive)	3.4 Mark 2 (automatic)	3.8 Mark 2 (overdrive)	3.8 Mark 2 (automatic)	240 (overdrive)	340 (overdrive)	Daimler 2½ V-8 (automatic)
Test source	*Autocar* 1965*	*Motor* 1962	*Motor* 1960	Autocar 1963	*Autocar* 1968	*Autosport* 1968	*Motor* 1963
Mean max speed (mph)	96.3	113.4	125	120.4	106	124	109.5
Acceleration (sec)							
0-30	5.7	4.5	3.2	3.6	4.1	3.5	4.8
0-40	8.5	6.4	4.9	5.3	6.3	—	7.0
0-50	12.7	9.0	6.4	7.2	9.3	6.9	9.6
0-60	17.3	11.9	8.5	9.8	12.5	8.8	13.5
0-70	23.8	15.3	11.7	12.9	16.4	—	18.4
0-80	33.3	20.0	14.6	16.9	22.8	16.6	24.2
0-90	49.9	26.0	18.2	21.3	31.0	—	31.8
0-100	—	33.3	25.1	28.2	44.8	26.4	42.3
0-110	—	44.5	33.2	37.0	—	—	—
Standing ¼-mile (sec)	20.8	19.1	16.3	17.2	18.7	17.2	19.8
Overall fuel consumption (mpg)	*Test of used car	16	15.7	17.3	18.4	17-22	16.4

	Daimler V-8 250 (overdrive)	3.4 S-type (overdrive)	3.8 S-type (overdrive)	3.8 S-type (automatic)	420 (overdrive)	420 (automatic)	Daimler Sovereign (automatic)
Test source	*Autosport* 1968	*Autocar* 1970*	*Motor* 1966	*Motor* 1965	*Autocar* 1967	*Motor* 1967	*CAR* 1968
Mean max speed (mph)	112	*Test of used car	121.1	116	123	115	118
Acceleration (sec)							
0-30	3.8	4.1	3.6	4.5	3.1	3.5	4.0
0-40	—	7.0	5.5	6.4	5.2	5.2	5.9
0-50	8.9	9.6	7.5	8.5	7.0	7.0	6.8
0-60	11.2	13.9	10.2	11.8	9.9	9.4	10.1
0-70	—	18.4	13.3	16.5	12.6	12.3	13.0
0-80	22.0	25.0	17.1	20.9	16.7	16.3	16.6
0-90	—	35.3	23.5	26.6	21.3	21.6	21.0
0-100	—	—	31.8	34.3	27.4	29.8	27.2
0-110	—	—	—	—	38.5	—	35.4
Standing ¼-mile (sec)	18.0	19.2	17.1	18.3	16.7	17.5	—
Overall fuel consumption (mpg)	18-22	14-17	15.4	15.3	16	15.4	15